ELIZABETH I

Also by Jacynth Hope-Simpson

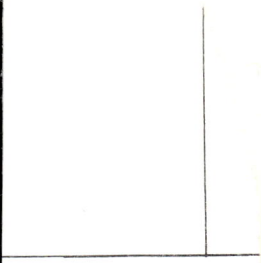

JACYNTH HOPE-SIMPSON

ELIZABETH I

HAMISH HAMILTON

LONDON

First published in Great Britain 1971
by Hamish Hamilton Children's Books Ltd
90 Great Russell Street, London, W.C.1
SBN 241 02032 8
Copyright © 1971 Jacynth Hope-Simpson
Printed in Great Britain by
Western Printing Services Ltd, Bristol

CONTENTS

SPAIN

FERDINAND = ISABELLA
of   of
ARAGON   CASTILE

JUANA
joint ruler
of
SPAIN

Catherine = (1) Arthur
of   = (2) HENRY
Aragon   VIII

(1) Catherine = HENRY VIII
of   m.
Aragon   (2) Anne Boleyn

CHARLES
V of
SPAIN,
Holy Roman
Emperor

FERDINAND I
Holy Roman
Emperor

PHILIP II = MARY I
of
SPAIN

ELIZABETH
I

PHILIP = (2) MARY
II of   I of
SPAIN   ENGLAND
        = (3) Elisabeth
              of
              France

Ferdinand
and Charles,
suitors of
Elizabeth

The Infanta
Isabel

ENGLAND   SCOTLAND

HENRY VII = Elizabeth of York.

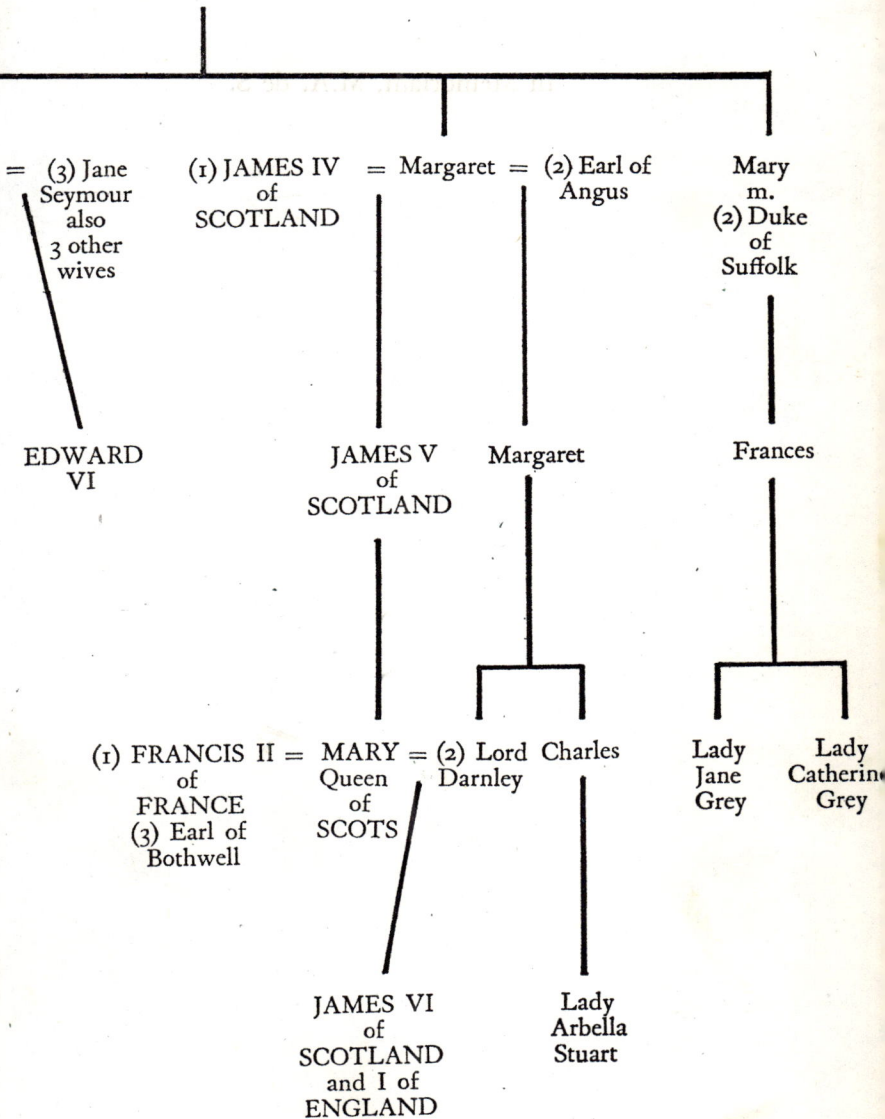

= (3) Jane
Seymour
also
3 other
wives

(1) JAMES IV
of
SCOTLAND

= Margaret =

(2) Earl of
Angus

Mary
m.
(2) Duke
of
Suffolk

EDWARD
VI

JAMES V
of
SCOTLAND

Margaret

Frances

(1) FRANCIS II =
of
FRANCE
(3) Earl of
Bothwell

MARY =
Queen
of
SCOTS

(2) Lord
Darnley

Charles

Lady
Jane
Grey

Lady
Catherine
Grey

JAMES VI
of
SCOTLAND
and I of
ENGLAND

Lady
Arbella
Stuart

In Memoriam, M.A. de S.

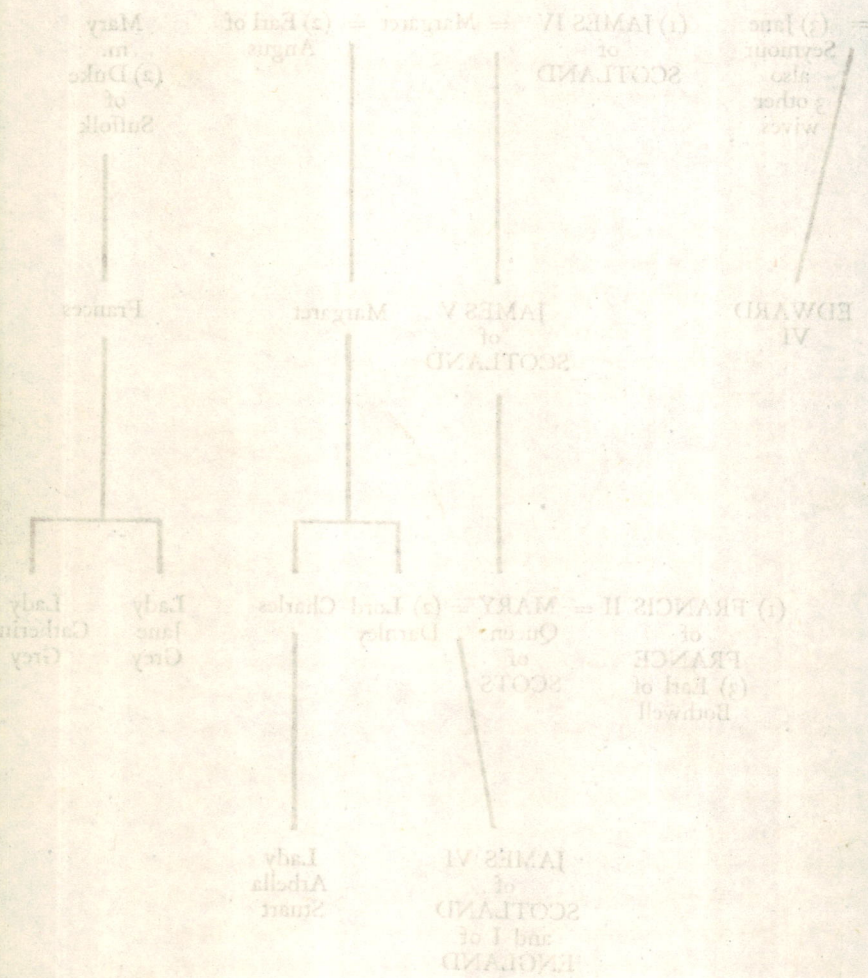

CHAPTER ONE

THE BEGINNING

"Thou art the rudeliest welcome to this world
That ever was prince's child."

Shakespeare, *Pericles, Prince of Tyre.*

The first action of her life was almost impossible to forgive. She was born a girl.

In any family in the kingdom, the birth of a girl as the first child of a marriage would have been disappointing. It was the year 1533, and then, and for centuries after, women had few legal rights. They existed mainly in relation to their fathers, and then their husband, rather than as individuals in themselves. Any family might have felt mildly cheated. How much worse when her father was the King of England himself.

Henry Tudor, the eighth Henry to reign in England, was forty-two years of age. He was then at a half-way mark. As a young man, he had been gay and glorious. His golden-red hair had gleamed in the sun, he had strode magnificently in velvet and satin and cloth of gold. He excelled at sports. As well as this, he had a lively intelligence, and wrote songs at one moment, theological argument at the next. Now time, and his own manner of life, were starting to lay their cruel hands upon him. The burnished hair was losing its sheen. A blur of fat was starting to bury his features. In the end, he would look like Claudius, whom Shakespeare called "the bloat King". Only his eyes, half obscured by fat, and the pads of his restless fingers, would give a hint of the lively mind still working within him.

But the young, god-like man had not yet become the grotesque that he was to be. He was still active, yet now, in middle-age, he longed desperately for a son who would take the throne after him.

Henry had first been married in 1509 to a Spanish girl, Catherine of Aragon. Her parents, Ferdinand and Isabella, were the joint rulers of Spain. They are known in Spain even today as "the Catholic Kings". Catherine, who was six years older than Henry, had been married before to his elder brother, Prince Arthur. When Arthur died, Henry inherited not only the succession to the throne but his brother's wife. The next twenty years were to be disappointing. Catherine bore her husband several children, but only one survived: a daughter, Mary, born in 1516. Henry did not want a daughter. Only one woman, Matilda, had reigned since the Norman Conquest, and she had been a disaster. More recently, within living memory, England had been torn by civil war for the lack of a clear male heir to the throne. For the sake of the country, as well as for his own satisfaction, Henry needed a son.

Each year, as his wife grew older, his hopes grew less. Nor did she have any attraction for him that could hold him to her in the face of his disappointment. Catherine was a devout and sincere, indeed an admirable, woman. She lacked beauty, gaiety, and vitality. Above all, she lacked youth, and Henry was now old enough to need reassurance that he was still young.

He asked himself why he, such an active and vigorous man, should be without a son, when the meanest ploughman in his kingdom could have male children in plenty. At last, he thought that he saw an answer. Catherine had been married before to his brother, Arthur. By the normal laws of the time, he could not have married her, but the

Pope had given permission. What if the Pope had been wrong? Henry remembered that the Bible declared, "And if a man shall take his brother's wife, it is an unclean thing . . . they shall be childless." Self-interest and religious scruples started to merge together. He began to consider putting Catherine away, and taking another wife. Then, at last, he might have a son.

His decision was to affect millions of lives. It happened at the moment when, after nearly 1500 years, the power of the Pope as head of the Christian church was under attack on many different levels. Europe was already beginning to split into the old Catholic and the new "Protestant" camps. Other men had defied the Pope, had been cast out from the Catholic church, and had survived. So, when the Pope refused to grant Henry a divorce from Catherine, Henry decided that he, too, would disown papal authority. The Pope would no longer be "Supreme Head" of the Church in England. Instead, he would be be so himself. Then he could legally marry another woman.

Of course, he had another woman in mind. The whole situation demanded it. Tragically, for her, the woman was Anne Boleyn.

Anne was no princess, as Catherine had been, but a waiting-woman at court, and the grand-daughter of a former Lord Mayor of London. With her lively black eyes and her slender neck, she had all the youth and vitality in which Catherine was so lacking. Henry was in a mood to fall as deeply in love as it was in his nature to do. Some said that she had bewitched him. Others, more superstitious, said that she was, in fact, a witch.

So this was the girl who now lay in her magnificent bed, and trembled because she had not borne the son whom the King demanded. The waiting-women wrapped the baby tight in her linen bands, and placed her in the cradle that had been decked out for a prince. Being women, they whispered to her that even if she were not a boy, she was still a pretty thing, and a sweeting.

In fact, she was not really prettty. As is often the way with young babies, she looked old, and remotely wise. It was as if she already knew things that would always puzzle her young mother. She seemed to have more control than her father, who was raging in vain for the son who had not been born.

The women looked at her again. That fuzz of red hair had come from her father, of course. There was no trace of him in her fine-boned wrists, or in a face which, even then, gave a hint she might be sharp-featured. One of them mentioned her grandfather, King Henry VII, and said she might look like him. They thought of that cunning and calculating Welshman, who had united a torn kingdom. Poor lass, she could do with a share of his wiliness.

Then the women hurried away, leaving her with her nurse. It was as well not to spend too much time with a child whom nobody wanted.

CHAPTER TWO

CHILDHOOD

"Pastime with good company
I love and shall until I die.
Grudge who list, let none deny!
So God be pleased, thus live will I."

King Henry VIII.

Gradually, she became aware of the world around her. As with all other children, the first world she knew was at the height of an adult's knee. It was dominated by greenery, for this was still an England of little cities and villages, of fields, formal gardens, and huge, wild expanses of woodland. The men who strode through this world were dressed in tight stockings and breeches, with a doublet falling to somewhere above their knees. The women, to small Elizabeth's view, were a stiff, long skirt that hid all the shape of the body beneath. The clothes, of both men and women, were in glowing, jewel-like colours. They were made of velvet and silk, often trimmed with fur. They looked soft and inviting to the child's hands, but if she tried surreptitiously to stroke them, she encountered the stiffness of gold thread embroidery, or the cold hardness of pearls.

Labour was cheap and counted for nothing, so life could be grand and splendid on a scale undreamt of today. Her early impressions were of pattern and ornament everywhere. There were carved panellings, carved furniture, embroidered hangings on walls and around huge beds. If she looked up, she saw carved and gilded plaster-work on the ceilings. On the floor level, near which her own life was still lived, things were less comfortable. Fierce draughts whistled over the flag-stones, and the cold seeped up through the rushes with which they were strewn. The heat of the log fires scorched when she went too near, but did not dispel the chill from the corners of large rooms. The magnificent houses smelt of the presence of too many human beings. Baths and drains had been forgotten in England since the Romans had left. At intervals, everyone might move on for a house to be purified. In the folds of their splendid garments, in the warmth of their unwashed bodies, they took their fleas away with them. Elizabeth accepted all the discomforts, for this was the only world that she knew. In the same way, a modern child will accept the noise, the fumes, and the constant danger of traffic.

On a personal level, life was very bewildering for the child. Once her father had accepted his disappointment that she was born a girl, he had made much of her. Henry, with his strong, out-going personality, could delight anyone when he chose. Elizabeth replaced her elder sister, Mary, as Princess of Wales. Mary was separated from her beloved mother, and ordered to wait on the child who had taken her place. But life could not continue untroubled for long when it depended on Henry's whims. He still yearned for a son, and Anne Boleyn showed no signs of producing one. As a young man he had written:

> As the holly groweth green,
> And never changeth hue,
> So I am, ever hath been
> Unto my lady true.

It was to be proved cruelly false.

Already Henry had started to look elsewhere. His

problem lay in the presence of two living wives. It was not much use having a son if people could claim that his third marriage was not legal. Catherine might die naturally, which would leave Anne to be disposed of. Then Anne told him that she was expecting another child. For the moment, she was reprieved. Catherine died, and three weeks later, Anne had a son. He was born prematurely, and born dead.

At this point, Henry pounced. He would find it easy enough to get rid of Anne. On her way to the throne, she had cared for nothing but to attract him. She had been too young and too light-hearted to make influential friends. Now there was nobody to protect her against the all-powerful king.

So Anne was sent to the Tower of London, accused of adultery with no less than five other men. To this day, no one knows if any of the charges was true. The accusations were enough to condemn the pretty and foolish girl. Once a poet, one of the men now accused with her, had likened her to a deer with a collar around her neck. On it was engraved in diamonds, "Do not touch me, for I am Caesar's." Now people remembered the ancient tag, that Caesar's wife must be above suspicion.

Anne went to the scaffold, fingering her white neck. She said that the headsman could cut through it easily, because it was so slender. Before she died, her fear turned to hysterical laughter, so that to some she seemed to be welcoming death. Next day, the King was betrothed to his third wife, Jane Seymour.

Elizabeth was then two years and eight months old. She was living in a separate house, so she would have had no sense of personal loss of her mother. It is hard to tell how she was affected emotionally when she later learnt how her mother had died. So many prominent people were executed at that time that she would have felt none of the shame that a child would feel today. Nor would she have felt the same physical horror. Physical suffering was an unescapable part of life. Women younger than Anne died in childbirth; many children did not live to grow up. All pain, from toothache to cancer, had to be endured without any anaesthetic. To be beheaded was only one part of the pattern of pain and death. So the shock would not sour and distort Elizabeth's life, as the shock of her mother's divorce had soured and distorted Mary's. It might well serve to make her cautious.

She was going to need to be. Now she, like Mary before her, was declared illegitimate. Her nurse, Lady Bryan, wrote in dismay to the Secretary of State, Thomas Cromwell:

"Now as my Lady Elizabeth is put from the degree (rank) she was in, and what degree she is now I know not but by hearsay, I know not how to order her or myself, or her women or grooms. I beg you to be good lord to her and hers, and that she may have raiment, for she has neither gown nor kirtle nor petticoat, nor linen for smocks, nor kerchiefs, sleeves. . . ."

The next year, Henry at last had the son he longed for. The birth of the child, Edward, killed his mother, Jane Seymour. Henry, delighted at having a son, had both his daughters to court. At Edward's christening, Mary was godmother, and Elizabeth bore a heavy christening robe. Because she was so little, she had herself to be carried. Henry was in a mood to do anything for his daughters; except admit they might have any claim to his throne.

With Jane dead, Henry was once again on the look-out for a wife. His fourth venture into matrimony provided the one moment of comedy in his unhappy affairs. Anne of Cleves was a Protestant German princess. An alliance with her would fit in well with Henry's feelings against the Pope, who was now even more of an enemy since Henry had abolished the monasteries. The marriage was duly arranged by Cromwell. Anne's beauty was vouched for by a portrait by Holbein which is now in the Louvre in Paris. When Henry saw the original of the portrait, he knew that he, for once, had been caught out. "What remedy?" he exclaimed in dismay at his first sight of "the Flanders Mare", to whom he was now committed. Within a few months, Anne was pensioned off, no doubt glad to have escaped so lightly. It was Cromwell who lost his head.

Henry now felt the need for a young and attractive wife. This time, it was Katherine Howard, a girl of about eighteen, who, like Anne Boleyn, was a niece of the Duke of Norfolk. Like Anne, she was thoughtless and light-hearted, and like Anne, she danced herself into the grave. Elizabeth was still only nine when Katherine went to the scaffold, accused of adultery. Her mother and her mother's cousin were now both dead. If this was where emotion led you, best learn to govern your feelings.

This sense of discipline was reinforced by Elizabeth's education. Nowadays, education is often "child-centred". The child's own interests and his own speed of learning dictate what he does. In the sixteenth century, the emphasis was much more on bringing the child up towards an ideal of excellence. This was done mainly by classical studies, and by a deep consideration of religious and moral questions. The child's own impulses were not given nearly as much importance as they would be given today.

So, by the time she was ten, Elizabeth had learnt Italian and French, and was grounded in Latin. At eleven, she translated a lengthy French poem, "The Mirror of a Sinful Soul". At fifteen, she was being taught by Roger Ascham, a brilliant young scholar from Cambridge. He made her translate Greek and Latin into English, and then back again into the original. He told a friend that she was "most eager. Her mind has no womanly weakness, her perseverance is equal to that of a man, and her memory long keeps what it quickly picks up. She talks French and Italian as well as she does English, and has often talked to me readily and well in Latin, moderately in Greek. When she writes Greek and Latin, nothing is more beautiful than her handwriting. She delights as much in music as she is skilful in it."

It is a convention to praise the already famous. In this case, it was deserved. Elizabeth's quickness of mind had been commented on ever since she was a small child. Her exquisite handwriting can still be admired today.

In this extraordinary childhood there were two obvious lacks: security and affection. At last, it began to look as if she might find both. Henry married again for what was to prove the last time. His new wife, Catherine Parr, was not a flighty young girl but a widow in her early thirties. Henry was aging rapidly, and her relation to him was partly that of a nurse. With true kindness and thoughtfulness, she brought the three children of such contrasted marriages together. Edward, the clever, pale-skinned, little boy was not much younger than Elizabeth, and could share in her education. Mary was now grown up. She still felt extremely badly about the way her father had treated her mother, but she was, at heart, a very affectionate woman. Her feelings flowed out to her young brother and sister, and she was known for the generosity of her gifts. For a time it looked as if they might at last know stability, in which Edward could grow up, marry, and himself have a son.

But Henry had lived too fiercely. Now, life was revenging itself on him. He became a swollen, panting caricature of his younger self. In 1547, when Elizabeth was thirteen and a half, he died.

CHAPTER THREE

EDWARD

"Woe to thee, O land, when thy king is a child."

Ecclesiastes.

King Edward VI is known to thousands of children who
go to King Edward's schools all over the country, and are
bidden at times to pray for "our pious founder, King
Edward VI". It is a fitting way to remember him. That
Edward actually founded these schools is sometimes disputed. That he was pious, there is no doubt at all, nor
that he had a passion for education. It is fitting, too, that
his name should still be associated with boys and girls of
his own age. In terms of a modern child's school life,
Edward came to the throne while still at primary school.
He died before he would have gone into the Sixth Form.

Obviously, a boy of nine cannot be given much freedom
to rule for himself. The man who actually took power
was his mother's brother, Edward Seymour. He was
created the Duke of Somerset, and took the name of
"Protector".

One problem which he inherited was the religious
one. Henry had broken with Rome while still begging
the question of what form the church in England was
going to take. Now there was increasing argument about
this. Many people wanted to keep the old Latin services
as Henry had done. Others wanted to follow the new
Protestant reformers, and to have services, with less
ceremony, said in English. Somerset's own chief concern

was to get uniformity for the sake of peace in the country. Edward himself had a precocious interest in theology, and under his last stepmother, Catherine Parr, had come into contact with Protestant sympathizers. It became clear that the new rulers would be on the side of reform.

So the Latin Mass was replaced by the first Book of Common Prayer, written in English. It was drawn up by Archbishop Cranmer, with the intention that it should be used at public worship by everybody in the country. As a compromise between old and new doctrines it reveals Cranmer's skill as a theological tight-rope walker. Some of the words he wrote are still used today, and they show he was one of the very greatest writers of English prose.

The split between the English church and Rome was becoming more apparent. The second Prayer Book of Edward's reign emphasized this, for it was more strongly Protestant both in teaching and forms of service. Nobody was more conscious of this than Edward's elder sister, Mary. She had been born and brought up in the faith of the Roman Catholic church. She believed in the supreme authority of the Pope in religious matters. She loved the old Latin services and the use of candles and incense, she believed in kneeling during a service as a part of worship. She liked images of the saints and the Virgin Mary. Now she was told to give all this up and to stop hearing Mass altogether. She replied with perfect sincerity, "May it please you to take away my life rather than the old religion." In the end, she had to hear Mass in secret, behind locked doors.

Meanwhile, Elizabeth's troubles were of a more personal nature. Somerset, the Protector, had a younger brother called Thomas Seymour. On Henry's death, Seymour wanted to secure his own position by marrying someone important. The obvious choice was one of the late King's daughters; Mary, or the thirteen-year-old

Elizabeth. Since nobody but himself showed any enthusiasm for the scheme, he did what seemed the next best thing, and married the King's own widow, Catherine Parr. Mary, remote in her determination to follow her own religion, retired to a separate household. Elizabeth went to live with her stepmother and with the man whom she might now be expected to look on as a substitute for her father.

Seymour duly continued Henry's tradition of leading a very unusual family life. It was not long before there was gossip about the way he would go into Elizabeth's room in his nightgown, while she was still in bed, and romp boisterously with her. Sometimes, his wife joined in. Once, she held Elizabeth tight while he cut the dress the girl was wearing to shreds. He may have hoped it to pass for horseplay, of the kind which a child would enjoy. But, as people were all too quick to remark, Elizabeth was no longer a child, and Seymour was notoriously attractive to women. The girl seemed to be both alarmed and excited by his behaviour. Then Catherine, who was expecting a child, became jealous. In order to silence gossip, Elizabeth was sent away. A few months later, she was told that Catherine had died in childbirth, the second of her stepmothers to do so.

Seymour's way seemed to be clear. He hoped to marry Elizabeth, who was now older than when he had first proposed it, and who, he knew well, was now strongly attracted to him. He also hoped to gain a personal power over Edward, who always enjoyed his company. Before he could act, the Privy Council, inspired by his own brother, the Protector Somerset, sent him to the Tower.

Suddenly, Elizabeth found herself in real danger. She might be accused of conspiring to marry Seymour in order to seize power with him. Young as she was, she knew all too well where accusations could lead. Her own mother had died on the scaffold with no real proof of her guilt. So had her young cousin, Katherine Howard. She would not be saved by her own royal blood, for she was reminded that she was "but a subject". As is the way at moments of crisis, the stories about her grew wilder. One even said that she had borne Seymour a child, which had been murdered at birth. More serious, it looked as if the evidence of her own servants might be distorted and used to implicate her.

Seymour was executed in March, 1549. Shortly before he died, he tried to have secret letters to Elizabeth and Mary smuggled out of the Tower. This was taken by some as a further sign that Elizabeth was concerned in his plots. Yet it was impossible to prove anything against her. She was able to give an answer to all charges, and showed considerable verbal skill for a girl of only fifteen and a half. When he died, her comment was strangely adult. "This day died a man of much wit, and very little judgement."

Was she really so detached, or was life rapidly teaching her the art of hiding her feelings? The daughter of Henry VIII and of Anne Boleyn might be expected to be an emotional woman. Seymour was the first man to have made her aware of this. She had been stirred, and frightened at the same time. Maybe, like her mother, she fingered her slender white neck.

Seymour did not fall alone. His brother, the Protector, was increasingly troubled by the economic problems of the country. A year after Seymour's death, he was ousted by John Dudley, later Duke of Northumberland. The reign suddenly took a different character, especially in religion. Edward, still only a boy of twelve, began to reveal himself as an ardent champion of Protestantism, who wished to purge from the church all traces of its connection with Rome. "If he lives," said the Bishop of Gloucester, "he will be the wonder and terror of the world."

This judgement suggests someone of considerably more force of character than the pale-faced, little prig that Edward is often thought of as being. However unlike he was to his father physically, Edward had inherited some of his father's fire. Just as it is easy to forget that the sensual Henry took delight in intellectual pastimes, so it can be forgotten that the studious Edward loved riding and shooting.

Elizabeth was not risking further trouble. She lived mostly away from court. She acquired a reputation for dressing simply, for being modest and fond of learning. There was no murmur of scandal to link her name with any man. Soon she would outlive the image of the wild and boisterous girl who had romped with Seymour. The party at court noted that, unlike Mary, she was a firm Protestant. She had need to be, when a whole country had changed its religious allegiance in order that she could be born.

It was a dull and limited life for a lively young girl in her late teens. It had the supreme virtue of being a safe one. Then, yet once again, the entire basis of Elizabeth's life was threatened. Edward had been taking an active part in state affairs while still being greatly occupied with his own education and normal boyish pursuits. Like his father, he was burning himself out, but it was happening very much younger. At the the age of fifteen, he died of consumption. No one can be certain what sort of king he would have become.

Now Henry's two daughters, both of whom had at times been declared illegitimate, were left as heirs to the throne. Normally, the elder girl, Mary, might have been expected to succeed automatically. But normal things did not happen in the atmosphere of high melodrama which ruled state affairs in those days. Northumberland wished to stay in power, but knew that Catholic Mary would never allow him to. So he took the desperate step of marrying his own son to Lady Jane Grey, the great-grand-daughter of Henry VII, and of proclaiming her Queen.

Elizabeth was summoned to London, but with her almost animal instinct for danger she stayed at Hatfield to ride out the storm. In less than a fortnight, it was all over. Mary, who had shown great personal courage, had come to the throne. Now it was Jane, Northumberland, and his son who were in the Tower. But with Mary the Catholic on the throne, Elizabeth the Protestant had trouble enough ahead.

CHAPTER FOUR

MARY

"Mary, Mary, quite contrary."

Nursery rhyme.

Of that gifted family, the Tudors, Mary was the only one who would have made a likeable next-door neighbour. She was a kind-hearted woman, very interested in people and their everyday affairs. She was especially fond of small children and babies. As a girl she had been quite pretty, but now, in her late thirties, she was dumpy and dull-complexioned. A Spaniard, seeing her for the first time, said, "She is a perfect saint and dresses badly." His comment would have hurt Mary. She was not nearly conceited enough to think of herself as a saint. As for dressing badly: she flattered herself on her very elaborate clothes, and everyone knew she loved bright, striking colours and shiny fabrics. The money she spent on finery was, indeed her chief weakness. Such was the affectionate, tragic woman who was to be one of the most hated rulers in all English history.

The heart of Mary's tragedy was her attachment to the Roman Catholic church. She had been brought up in its faith, and she had clung to its faith through all the troubles of her mother's divorce and her father's re-marriages. At one point, she had given in, and admitted in writing that, whatever the Pope had said, her parents had never been legally married. The shame of this surrender was to mark her for life. Never again would she give way. After all, she was the grand-daughter of Ferdinand and Isabella who had finally conquered the Mohammedan Moors in Spain. If they had saved Spain for the Church, surely she could save England?

Anyone sensitive to political atmosphere might have noticed signs that England did not want to be saved. Already a whole generation had grown up since the time when England had rejected the authority of the Pope. The idea had spread that Englishmen, and Englishmen only, should be responsible for their own affairs. Fortunes had been built up, and noble families founded, on the money obtained when the monasteries were suppressed. As for the clergy, many of them had acquired wives whom the Roman Catholic church would never acknowledge.

Against this background, Mary set out to find a husband. She needed a king to help govern, and now, once again, the problem of an heir to the throne had become vital. She could not endure that the Protestant Elizabeth should succeed her. True, Elizabeth on her knees, and with tears in her eyes, had begged to be instructed in the Catholic faith. For a happy moment, Mary had believed her. With her simple clothes, and her red-gold hair neatly smoothed, Elizabeth looked a pattern of pious girlhood. Then after a few weeks, she had stopped coming to Mass. Mary, agonizingly sincere herself, was forced to wonder if her conversion was just a pretence. There was another Elizabeth: a girl with a cloud of hair floating flame-like about her face, a girl who loved dancing, and could fascinate men. Mary reminded herself that Elizabeth's mother had been, at least in Catholic eyes, a liar and a wanton.

One obvious husband for Mary would have been her own kinsman, Edward Courtenay. Courtenay might not have very much to recommend him personally, but he did have the one great advantage of being an Englishman.

Instead of him, Mary's choice fell on her cousin's son, Philip, heir to the throne of Spain. Being half Spanish herself, she thought him a natural choice. With her lack of political awareness, she did not stop to ask herself how he would strike her subjects. For English feeling was outraged at the idea of having a Spaniard set over them. Down in the far south-west, the Mayor and aldermen of Plymouth even went so far as to ask for their town to be put under French protection.

Then rebellion broke out in Kent. Mary had to remove anybody who might be a threat to her throne. Lady Jane Grey, the Queen for twelve days, was still in the Tower, for Mary's natural instinct had been to be merciful to her. Now she was executed. This left Elizabeth, who was suspected of having encouraged the rebels. She was brought to London and ruthlessly cross-examined. With the same cool-headed skill that she had shown during the Seymour crisis, she staved off all the questions. It was impossible to prove any charge against her. She herself was said to have scratched on a window pane:

> Much suspected of me,
> Nothing proved can be,
> Quoth Elizabeth, prisoner.

Even so, there was enough suspected for her to be sent to the Tower.

When Elizabeth was told where she was going, she was aghast. Her mother and cousin had gone to the Tower, and never come out alive. It was only a few weeks since Jane Grey, a clever and gentle girl even younger than herself, had lost her head there as well. There seemed little hope. She begged to be allowed to write an appeal to her sister, Mary.

Even at this frightening moment, Elizabeth's cool and decisive brain was working. They would have to take her down to the Tower by barge, for the Thames was still the main highway in London. She knew it was only possible to shoot through the narrow arches of London Bridge on an out-going tide. If she could delay things a little, the tide would turn. So she wrote on and on, protesting her innocence. Her invention started to flag, and the exquisite handwriting became scratchy. The men standing behind her grumbled impatiently. At last, she had to stop, but most of her second side was still blank. What if somebody forged a confession of guilt on it? Once again, her wits did not fail her. She drew long diagonal lines all over the blank paper, and then signed her name on the bottom. The tide had turned. She had gained a day, but it was only a day.

Next morning, Palm Sunday, was damp and cloudy. Elizabeth was taken down river to the watergate of the Tower. It is now known as the "Traitors' Gate". When she arrived, the river was running so high over the steps, that she could not get out of the barge without soaking her feet. The lesser worry combined with her greater dread, and for a time she refused to move. When she finally entered the Tower, she cried out in alarm at the sight of the armed guard. Although she was told they were not for her, she would not believe the assurance. "I know it is so, it needeth not for me, being, alas! but a weak woman." This was to be a favourite line of defence from one who proved a match for any man living.

While Elizabeth was in danger, Mary was in a dilemma. She had found no proof with which to condemm Elizabeth to death, and to execute her might spark off rebellion throughout the country. Yet she could not let Elizabeth loose to become a focus for discontent. As a compromise, she sent her off to a form of house-arrest at Woodstock. Here, Elizabeth chafed impatiently. The only outlet for her energies was to torment her gaolers, in which she showed considerable skill and ingenuity. Even so, it was not enough for a girl in the full eagerness of her youth, who, like a young eagle, was starting to sense her own exceptional powers.

Meawhile, Philip of Spain came to England to marry Mary. He had been advised to bring his own doctors and cooks to England in case he should be poisoned. It was scarcely a happy prospect. When he arrived, he found people sullen or downright hostile: with one important exception. On meeting her bridegroom for the first time, Mary fell deeply in love.

She was a very affectionate woman who had never had a full outlet for her affections. Her father had been changeable, her mother had been taken from her and died. Her little brother, Edward, had died as well. There was, of course, still Elizabeth, but relations between them were scarcely normal. At the best of times, loving Elizabeth was like loving a will o' the wisp. All her dammed-up affection was now poured out on to the politely bewildered Philip. He was not even a very lovable person, although he was later to show an attractive side of his character to the daughters of a subsequent marriage. But love is notoriously blind. To Mary, it was enough that he was hers.

Mary imagined that she had achieved personal happiness. Only two things remained. One was to restore her country to the Roman Catholic church. That she did, and Parliament duly declared itself "very sorry and repentant" for the break with Rome. The other was for her to bear an heir to the throne. That also, Mary had grounds to believe she was going to do. For a few days, life seemed perfect to her. She was completely lacking in that power, which Elizabeth, so much younger, had already shown, to sense the true nature of a situation. It never even occurred to her that she stood on the brink of disaster.

For England showed no great wish to be Catholic. As ever, in all human affairs, motives were very mixed. There were those who genuinely believed in the new forms of religion, as fervently and sincerely as Mary believed in the old ones. There were those who identified the Protestant faith with national independence. Then, as always in difficult times, there were those who would ally themselves with any protestors simply out of a wish to cause trouble. The government did not stop to disentangle motives. They fell back on the established punishment for heretics. They burnt them alive.

So the market places of England were made hideous by the stench of human flesh. It was one of the most ghastly errors in English history, and the memory still lives on. It can be argued that Catholics had been martyred by Henry VIII and that more were to die in the future. It can be argued that Mary herself was not wholly responsible. In so far as she was, she was moved by a sense of duty, and certainly not by any delight in shedding blood. But no attempt to be reasonable does away with the fact that Mary earned for herself the name of "Bloody" Mary, and that this name has lasted for four hundred years. It was she, in her innocent simple-mindedness, who kindled the hatred between Christians of different denominations which still exists in some places in Britain today.

At the same time, personal tragedy was waiting for Mary. Everything had been made ready for the birth of her child, but now people began to wonder if she was really pregnant at all. Had she misinterpreted her symptoms, or were those symptoms the product of her almost hysterical longing for an heir? Finally, she acknowledged that there was no hope of a child. Philip went back to Spain.

The rest of her life was disastrous. The country was uneasy. Philip was absent for nearly two years, and she knew he did not share her own feeling for him. When he returned, she believed herself pregnant again, but once again it was delusion. There was nothing to show

for his return, except that he got her to help in his war
with France. As a result, England lost Calais, her last
remaining continental possession.

In 1558, Mary died, at the age of forty-two. Early in
the next century, a preacher was to refer to her as "a good
woman, as they say, but an ill prince". It was a fair
judgement on this unhappy woman.

Now, out of all Henry's efforts to get an heir, there
was only Elizabeth left.

CHAPTER FIVE

THE THRONE

"When I was fair and young, and favour gracèd me,
Of many was I sought, their mistress for to be;
But I did scorn them all, and answered them therefore,
'Go, go, go, seek some otherwhere,
Importune me no more'."

Queen Elizabeth I.

So Elizabeth Tudor became Queen of England Etc.

Et cetera was a somewhat unusual title. It replaced the
phrase "Head of the Church" which her father and
brother, but not, of course, her sister Mary, had used.
Did she intend to be head of the Church? This simply
showed that the girl believed in keeping everyone waiting.

She came to London to show herself to her people.
On a cold Saturday in January, 1559, she went in triumph
through the City of London. She was carried on a litter,
or small platform, dressed in heavy cloth of gold. The
litter was canopied, and the sides draped with gold
brocade. It glowed against the deep red damask and
velvet of her attendants. The flurries of snow and the
sullen sky only made it gleam the brighter by contrast.

She processed through the narrow, crowded streets of
the city. The upper storeys of the tall houses jutted out
over the lower ones, and cut the pale winter light. All
around, everybody was cheering wildly. From place to
place, there were tableaux and pageants, representing
the rule of King Henry VIII and the happy times

that Elizabeth's reign would bring forth. Somehow she aroused, from the start, an instinct within the nation for display and for drama. She inspired it, and everyone felt she was joining in.

For the girl who now went through the city was as skilful an actor as any in the plays that she saw. She expressed at the same time royalty, and a joy in the love of her people. Apart from all her elaborate costume, she was a striking person. Her figure was very slender. In an age when the dress of both men and women was artificially bulky, her natural lightness and grace made her conspicuous. Her colouring was dramatic. Her red-gold hair floated above a pale, almost pallid, face. There is no suggestion, in any description of her, that her skin, like that of so many red-heads, was freckled. Her eyes were light in colour, but strangely intense. If she lived to be old, she would become short-sighted.

Of course, as she rode through the City, and again on the next day when she was crowned, everyone said she was beautiful. None of her portraits suggest that she really was. But she had the far more important gift for a queen of being able to project herself. When she wanted to, she could enchant people. Someone said of her, "When she smiled, it was a pure sunshine." When she danced, and she loved to dance, she was like a moving flame.

She was young. She was magnetic. She was Queen in her own right of a small but fiercely independent nation. On any reckoning, she was the most eligible woman in Europe. Happy the man who would become her husband.

It was obvious that she would marry. She needed a man whose knowledge and judgement would help her to govern. The mere fact of his being a man would, of course, make him more skilful at statecraft than she could ever hope to be. Then she would want to marry.

There was no sign that she hated masculine company;
very much the reverse. Above all, the old cry came, she
must marry to have an heir.

At present, the heir to the throne was yet another young
woman. She was the grand-daughter of Henry VIII's
sister Margaret, who had married the King of Scotland.
Her name was Mary Stuart. She was not only Queen of
Scotland in her own right, but was married to the
young heir to the throne of France. Naturally, no one in
England wished to be ruled by France. Elizabeth had
better get married at once. Then, after fifty unhappy
years, there might at last be a legitimate male heir to the
throne. The thoughts of England turned longingly to a
small, red-headed Harry bawling lustily in his cradle.
All that was needed was for Elizabeth to get married, and
that was a mere technicality.

The suitors began to line up. The first was, of all
people, her own brother-in-law, Mary's husband, Philip
of Spain. He implied that he would be doing England
a very great favour. He would save the country from
reverting to Protestantism, and he would be an ally
against France. Elizabeth showed signs of interest.
Most people were horrified, for they had already had
more than enough of Philip, and they still showed a
strange reluctance to be saved from their own errors.
Then they began to wonder what Elizabeth was up to.
Was Philip simply a smoke-screen to keep the Pope and
the English Catholics quiet, while Parliament declared
that England was Protestant once again? Soon, she
had turned him down flat. Although Philip had never
really wanted to marry her, he felt aggrieved about this.
Elizabeth, he suggested, would never be able to hold
her own against France unless Spain were to help her.
The wilful, inconstant Elizabeth was not distressed.
Could it even be that she had calculated that Spain
could never hold her own against France without the

help of England? Philip was bound to her by their shared interest, whether he liked it or not.

The next row of suitors moved in. There was the son of the King of Sweden, an uncouth young man. Some observers suggested he might be an imbecile. It was feared this might not recommend him to a self-willed young woman, who seemed to be rather fussy. She had even declared, quite against the normal custom for royalty, that she would not marry a man she had never seen. Perhaps she remembered her father and Anne of Cleves.

Then Philip's two cousins, younger sons of the Emperor Ferdinand, were, so to speak, dangled before her. The young men were, in the nature of things, foreigners, and her sister's unhappy experience did not draw her towards a foreign marriage. She was already making capital in the country out of the fact that she was "descended by father and mother of mere English blood". Besides, they were Catholics. Elizabeth was clearly a Protestant. On opening her first Parliament, she had dismissed the monks who met her in broad daylight with lighted candles. "Away with those torches. We can see well enough." Yet, even as Protestant hearts rejoiced, Elizabeth brought out candles and a crucifix, according to Catholic custom, in her own private chapel. How could you possibly know where you stood with a woman like that?

The only hope was to marry her to an Englishman. No one quite liked to voice the thought that only an Englishman would be able to deal with her. All the sensible, middle-aged men who imagined themselves as advisors to this capricious young female looked round for a suitable candidate. Elizabeth's only reaction was to declare she would never marry and that words to that effect must be cut on her tombstone. Naturally, no one took any notice. They drew some comfort from the fact that she admitted she was "only human and sensible to human emotions and impulses". She said she might one day change her mind and marry for the good of the kingdom, "or it might be for other reasons". Then suddenly, the whole situation changed. Without asking anyone for advice, without stopping to question the common sense of her choice, the Queen had fallen in love.

However hard she had tried, she could scarcely have chosen anyone worse. He was Lord Robert Dudley, a son of that Duke of Northumberland who had died on the scafford for trying to put Lady Jane Grey on the throne. His whole family had been described as "a tribe of traitors". He was Master of the Horse in Elizabeth's household: her "horse-keeper", said Mary Queen of Scots contemptuously, as if to imply he were little more than a groom. All this might be bad enough, but, to make things worse, he was married.

It was not as if he had qualities to make up for these glaring faults. True, he was charming and handsome, a skilful horseman, and a fascinating talker. All this appealed strongly to the daughter of Henry VIII and of Anne Boleyn. Her natural physical liveliness made it likely that she would love someone like that. But Elizabeth's husband would have to be King of England, and a king ought to be more than a gifted rider. Nobody was convinced that Dudley had any qualities which would fit him for the position, even if his wife had not been alive. It was now ten years since the scandal about Seymour, but in many ways the two men were alike. Both were active, handsome, lively, and superficially charming. Was it Elizabeth's fate to fall in love with men of this type, who in intellect and strength of character were no real match for herself?

Rumours flew around Europe. Soon, they were downright scandalous. How great was the intimacy between the Queen and Dudley? At one moment, she was behaving like a love-sick girl, much younger than her twenty-five years. Once, she even dressed up as a servant maid in order to be near him. Then, next moment, she became entirely a Queen, as frightening in her dignity and sudden rages as ever her father had been. Mrs Ashley, who had served her since her childhood, and who had been with her all through the Seymour scandal, begged her, on her knees, to consider her reputation. What chance, asked Elizabeth tartly, had she to be immoral, with so many attendants around her night and day? But, she added, with a mixture of queenliness and pure acid, if she did want "a dishonourable life", she "did not know of anyone who could stop her".

Scandal grew. Nearly everyone, apart from the Queen herself, saw Dudley as only an unscrupulous adventurer who would stop at nothing in order to marry her. There were rumours that his wife, Amy Robsart, had cancer. When, seven months later, she was still alive, the Spanish ambassador wrote home to Philip that Dudley was planning to poison his wife with the Queen's silent consent. The situation was made worse since Mary of Scotland had now become Queen Consort of France as well. If Elizabeth would not marry and have an heir, Mary would in due course, become Queen of England. England would then be no more than a satellite of France.

Amidst all her own affairs, the problem of France and Scotland was occupying Elizabeth's mind. Scotland was a Protestant country, far more fervent and extreme than she was herself. It was garrisoned by Roman Catholic Frenchmen. Suddenly the Scots rose against their French masters. It soon became clear that they would not succeed in driving them out on their own, and they appealed to Elizabeth to help them. This meant she would have to commit herself, one way or the other. Elizabeth had already shown that committing herself was just what she hated doing.

Apart from the marriage problem, it was her first

real test as a diplomat. She handled it delicately. All the negotiations with the Scots were conducted by her principal Secretary, William Cecil. Cecil had been a friend of hers ever since she was fourteen, and she was rumoured to have selected him as her chief minister even before Mary's death. The choice shows her brilliant judgement of men: provided that they were not the type of men that she fell in love with. Fortunately for England, Cecil was not. He was intelligent, conscientious, a master of detail, and a man of principle and integrity; in short, the ideal public servant. As such, he was to be much more important to England than any of the glamorous young men who took the Queen's fancy.

While he dealt, very capably, with the Scots, Elizabeth talked to the foreign diplomats in London. Cecil was still rather doubtful about letting her do this. Matters of weight he declared, were "too much for a woman's knowledge". Unfortunately, no foreign ambassador could speak English. Elizabeth could speak Latin as fluently as himself, and French and Italian much better. So he had to allow her to play her part in charming and cajoling the foreign envoys. Perhaps she could use her feminine wiles to mislead them a little as well. It was still the stage when no one was taking Elizabeth as a ruler quite seriously. The Spanish ambassador had some idea of the truth when he had called her, before she came to the throne, "a very vain woman but a very acute one". Later, when she was queen, he remarked, she "gives her orders and has her way as absolutely as her father did". Not even he foresaw, in these early days, that she would end up by conducting more of her own diplomacy than any king of her day.

Between them, Elizabeth and Cecil concealed their true intentions. They were able to send an army to Scotland before France could raise forces to stop them. At first, things did not go well. To Cecil's horror,

Elizabeth showed signs in private of wanting peace and of hating spending money. Both were reactions with which he later grew all too familiar. Then the French indicated that they were ready to negotiate, and Cecil went off to Scotland. He came home in July, 1560, having concluded the Treaty of Edinburgh. All French forces would be withdrawn from Scotland. England need no longer fear invasion by her back door. The treaty also recognized Elizabeth's right to the English throne, and pledged the rulers of France and Scotland not to lay claim to her title. No one was sure yet if Mary Queen of Scots would accept the treaty. What it had done, so far as the people of Scotland were concerned, was to form a new link with England in place of the old link with France.

In Europe, the Treaty was looked on as a diplomatic triumph. It was, of course, the result of the partnership between Elizabeth and Cecil, which was to become one of the great partnerships in history. The world at large was inclined to give Elizabeth most of the credit, as being the more striking figure. She was young, she was fascinating, now she had proved she was very clever as well. All over Europe, people waited to see what would happen next. It was not long before there was another sensation about her. In the September of 1560, Robert Dudley's wife was found dead in an empty house.

It was natural to suspect murder. Few people trusted Dudley, and Elizabeth, after all, was the child of Henry VIII who had killed and divorced without scruple to get the women he wanted. All the world knew for certain was that Amy Robsart had sent the servants out for the day. For a woman in her social position to be alone in a house was more unusual at that time than it would be now. She had then been discovered, dead, at the foot of a staircase. The commonest story was that her neck was broken. To this day, there is still a mystery as to what happened. One likely explanation is that she was driven to suicide by her husband's neglect.

Whatever the rights and wrongs of the matter, Elizabeth's situation was desperate. Dudley was now a free man, and one part of her complex nature longed to marry him. Yet to do so, might make her seem party to Amy's death, and be disastrous to her as a queen. Her path to the throne had been a difficult one, requiring great caution. Now she was Queen, she found that she had a taste for royalty and for ruling. Should she throw all this away? Would she get anything in return? Her mother and her sister, Mary, had only found disaster in loving.

Could she hope to marry Dudley and ride out the scandal? Something else held her back. The young Scottish diplomat, James Melville had said to her, "You think if you married you would be but Queen of England, and now you are King and Queen both." This was, and would always remain, the heart of her dilemma.

Yet while Elizabeth might not marry Dudley, she would not send him away from court. If she did so, it would be taken as proof that she thought him guilty of Amy's murder. She did not believe that he was. The situation appeared dangerously near boiling point. Elizabeth's answer was typical of herself. While all the gossips in Europe assumed she would either marry him or disown him, she took the heat out of the matter by doing precisely nothing at all.

CHAPTER SIX

THE RIVAL

"We are both in one isle, both of one language, both the nearest kinswoman that each other hath, and both Queens."

Mary Stuart of herself and Elizabeth Tudor.

There was no one on earth like her, and she rejoiced in the fact. She was a woman, and she was young, and she was a queen. She was slender and graceful, and her bright hair gleamed like the sun. Her skin was pale, and the veins in it showed delicately, with the Tudor blood running through them. She knew, for so many people had told her, that she was alluring to men. The woman who looked in her glass and saw all this was called Elizabeth Tudor. She was also called Mary Stuart.

Mary was Elizabeth's first cousin once removed, which may have accounted for their likeness in colouring. Her great-grandfather was Elizabeth's grandfather, Henry VII. Her grandfather and father had both been kings of Scotland. She herself had become Queen of Scotland when she was only six days old. Scotland was a troubled, uneasy country for a young child. It was made worse by the fact that Henry VIII wished to unite the two kingdoms by marrying her to his young son, Edward. The Scots, distrusted Henry, felt that it would be safer to send their little queen out of the country. At the age of six years she was sent to her mother's homeland of France and was brought up with the French royal children.

In France, she had an idyllic childhood. The French court was elegant and well-mannered, fond of music and dancing and all the graces of life. It processed from great house to great house that all had the quality of a dream or a fairy-tale. There was Fontainbleau, in its stag-haunted forest that looked like the background to a mediaeval tapestry. There were gleaming chateaux set by the river Loire, with turrets and winding staircases that were exciting for a small child. When their surroundings palled, there were plenty of other things to amuse the children. Actors and acrobats came to entertain them. There was a positive menagerie of pet animals for them to play with. The royal cooks vied with each other to make them exotic sweets. All the time, there was companionship and affection.

Nothing could have been further from the bleak world of Elizabeth Tudor. In infancy, she had been branded a bastard and had known her mother beheaded. In adolescence, she had been roughly awakened by the mingled attraction and threat of Seymour's advances. Mary sailed in state down the Loire, in a large barge ornamented with richly embroidered cloth. In another barge, nearby, the court musicians were playing. Elizabeth had sailed down the Thames, and then shivered in waking nightmare, ankle-deep in water at the Traitor's Gate of the Tower.

When she was fifteen years old, Mary married the Dauphin Francis, the young heir to the French throne, with whom she had been brought up. Next year he became King of France. Mary was thus Queen twice over, of Scotland by birth and of France by marriage. More, she quartered the English arms on her coat of arms as if to lay claim to be Queen of England as well. Her future looked dazzling. Then in 1560, at the age of not quite seventeen, Francis died.

Mary was grief-stricken. Francis does not appear to have been an attractive or lovable person, but to her this was the first crumbling of her happy, familiar world. She put on the white which was court mourning in France. It made her tall, slender figure appear even lighter, and made her eyes more luminous in her pale face. As she walked up and down the alleys of the great garden of of Fontainbleau, her long veil was caught by the wind, and billowed around her, like a barque in full sail. The famous French poet, Ronsard, stood watching her as she walked, and captured the moment for ever.

Perhaps it was while she was walking at Fontainbleau that Mary made up her mind to go back to Scotland. From the moment she made her decision, her life became entwined with Elizabeth's. They were to be linked together in a strange intimacy that could only end when one or the other died.

Their first encounter was when Mary asked permission to travel through England on her way back to Scotland. Elizabeth refused. Her grounds were that Mary had never signed the Treaty of Edinburgh, whereby she had been asked to renounce her claims to the English throne. This was a vital point to Elizabeth because, in the eyes of some Catholics who had never acknowledged Henry's marriage to Anne Boleyn, Mary had a better claim than herself.

So, in the dull, misty weather of a wretched August, Mary was forced to take the long sea-route to Scotland. She tossed her way through seas infested by pirates, and patrolled by Elizabeth's ships. Her admirers were indignant. They contrasted Mary, the virtuous Queen Dowager of France, with Elizabeth, whose behaviour with Dudley had recently been the biggest scandal in Europe.

When Mary reached Scotland, it seemed like a different world from the one she had left. The very sky over her head, wind-swept and rain-racked, looked different from in France. The nobles who came to meet her seemed more like the chiefs of some savage tribe than the

polished courtiers with whom she had dealt in the past.
The very horses of her procession were poorer than she
was used to. As she drove into Edinburgh, she saw
wretched hovels, where people struggled to live in a cold,
damp climate. In the city itself, the houses were tall,
almost cliff-like buildings of bleak grey stone, with layer
upon layer of human beings packed into them. Dark,
mysterious alleyways led into courtyards and closes beyond.

Dominating the city, were two jagged hills. At the
foot of the bigger one, Arthur's seat, lay the Palace of
Holyroodhouse. The Scots showed it proudly to Mary,
for it was magnificent by their standards of that time. To
her, its stone floors and wood-panelled walls, its com-
paratively small rooms must have appeared provincial
and rather oppressive.

"Fires of joy" were lit to welcome her. That night,
several hundred musicians played on their fiddles and
rebecs and sang psalms. The sophisticated ear of a French
courtier noticed they sang out of tune.

But whatever her personal feelings, Mary had come to
Scotland anxious to please. So far in her life she had
found the fact that she was an attractive and charming
woman was more than enough. In Scotland, she was
suddenly faced with problems completely outside her
experience. The Scots, reputation abroad was as a nation
of brave fighters. Now she found that they carried this
over into their lives at home. The whole country was
disordered and lawless. The nobles, on whom she had
hoped to depend, had little thought beyond advancing
their own family interests, normally at the expense of any
other nobles around. In many ways, the country was
still almost primitive, with a widespread belief in witch-
craft and black magic.

When the voice of the church was raised, it was in an
accent that Mary could not understand. Almost exactly

a year before her return, the Scottish Parliament had declared the country Protestant. It had abolished the power of the Pope, and had made celebrating Mass punishable by death for a third offence. Compared to the English Reformation, which grew out of political circumstances, the Scottish Reformation was a passionate and violent thing. It had no truck with a middle way between Catholicism and extreme reform such as Cranmer and later Elizabeth tried to tread.

Mary herself was a Catholic by birth and by upbringing. Her temperament was quite moderate, and she had come to Scotland assuming that if she gave her subjects freedom to practise their religion, she would have the same freedom to practise her own. On her first Sunday in Scotland, she found out that she was wrong. When news came that Mass was being said in her private chapel, the citizens of Edinburgh started to demonstrate. There were shouts and threats of violence. In the end, the chapel door had to be guarded. Inside, the priest was so terrified that he could hardly raise his hands to elevate the Host.

All too soon, Mary encountered the apostle of the Scottish Reformation, the vehement John Knox. Knox was a man who had suffered for his opinions. For a time, he had been condemned to row as a slave in the French galleys. He was prepared to make others suffer as well.

In Knox's eyes, Mary had two grievous faults. The first was that of being a Catholic, which to his way of thinking made her an ally of Satan. The second was even worse, since nothing at all could be done about it. She was a woman.

Knox was prepared to admit that women served some limited useful purpose when strictly confined to the home. He considered they were as a race, "weak, frail, impatient, feeble and foolish creatures", and were automatically inferior to men. The idea that women should ever be set over men in authority was "more than a monster in nature". When Mary Tudor had come to the throne he had expressed his views with great vehemence in a book called *First Blast of the Trumpet against the Monstrous Regiment of Women*. "Regiment" here means government by women. Now that he was faced with a Queen set in authority over himself, he went on expressing his views with still greater passion.

There was perhaps one woman on earth who could have made Knox hold his tongue. That was Elizabeth. As her Councillors had now learnt, she was intellectually formidable, and she revelled in long theological arguments. If that had failed, she could have been at least as rude to Knox as he would have been to her. Among the things that she had inherited from her father were his violent rages and an astonishing flood of truly hair-raising language.

Mary stood no chance against Knox. She tried looking charming, which had no effect whatsoever. Then she tried a little mild argument. Mary was quite a cultured woman with a taste for French poetry and mediaeval romances. Knox merely thought her silly. In the end she fell back on woman's ultimate weapon, tears. So far from being moved, Knox ungallantly called this "howling".

Elizabeth from afar heard reports of all this with an interest not entirely untinged by malice. Soon there were rumours that Mary was looking out for a husband. In the general masculine view, she was behaving better than Elizabeth ever had in the same situation. In the first place, she had no encumbrances in the form of a Dudley. In the second place, she seemed to care for nothing but needs of state. She was prepared to marry Don Carlos, heir to Philip II. He was known to be epileptic, suspected to be insane, and was so undersized that he weighed only five stone. What a contrast to Elizabeth and her notorious weakness for good-looking men.

The two women had not yet met. Mary was disappointed. Knowing that she could charm most people, short of John Knox, she felt that a meeting would improve their relationship. Elizabeth would have agreed, but a religious war broke out in France between Catholics and the Huguenots, or French Protestants. The moment did not seem right. In the meantime, Elizabeth tried to satisfy her curiosity as to what this romantic paragon really was like. She questioned everyone who had seen Mary, and her interest in Mary's appearance became almost obsessive. The best news, from her point of view, was that Mary was over five foot eleven tall; tall for a woman at any time, and especially so in those days. That was over-tall for a queen, said Elizabeth waspishly.

As if to show that no queen could rival herself, Elizabeth dressed with amazing elaboration. She glittered and shone when she moved. All her portraits show her in stiff dresses, thickly encrusted with jewels. It was a vision of royalty designed to dazzle her subjects. In contrast, Mary's portraits show dresses with simpler, more fluid lines, and a taste for plain black and white, even when she was not in mourning. It might be argued that Mary's clothes show the greater confidence in her appearance.

This purely feminine jealousy of Mary seemed to occupy a large part of Elizabeth's mind. At the same time, Elizabeth was considering Mary more coolly and analytically. She knew that there would be pressure on her to recognize Mary as the heir to the throne. This, she thought, would be dangerous. If there was a recognized heir, somebody might try to remove herself.

When Mary sent an envoy, asking to be recognized, Elizabeth saw him in the presence of Cecil and Dudley. She made a great show of surprise.

"The desire is without example to require me in my own life, to set my winding sheet before my eyes. Think you that I could love my own winding sheet? Princes cannot like their own children, those that should succeed to them. .... How then shall I, think you, like my cousin, being declared my Heir Apparent?"

She spoke with some feelings of the problems that she had experienced as heir to her sister Mary. "I know the inconstancy of the people of England, how they ever mislike the present government and have their eyes fixed on that person who is to succeed." She pointed out that there would be dangers for Mary as well as herself. She added, in Latin, "They are more prone to worship the rising than the setting sun."

Elizabeth might dismiss the problem, but her advisers were very worried. It was becoming increasingly clear that, the Dudley complication apart, Elizabeth was reluctant to do her duty to the country by marrying and producing an heir. Then, in October 1562, she fell very ill with smallpox. For a week, she hovered between life and death, unaware of the world around her. She did not know that, in nearby rooms, her ministers were talking in hushed voices. Who was there who could succeed her? Could anyone take the throne without having to fight for it? The stability of the country, which Henry VII and then Henry VIII had established, was more precious than anything else.

At that moment too, there was some glimmering of how much the continuing stability of the country had owed to Elizabeth. The young woman now tossing and moaning with fever was not simply a figurehead, but an active political force. After the unhappy reigns of her brother and sister, she had brought back confidence in the firm rule of the Tudors.

In the end, Elizabeth, with her strong instinct for survival, fought off disease. She only just won. "Death", she admitted, "possessed almost every part of me." When she was able to look in a mirror, she saw that she had been scarred. She was worried lest she look older, for in those days a woman was thought middle-aged at thirty. She pointed out angrily to the House of Commons that "the marks they saw on her face were not wrinkles but pits of smallpox".

The Commons were taking what Elizabeth felt was an over-zealous interest in her affairs. Like her Council, they wanted to know who was to succeed her. Elizabeth sent them a letter upon the subject. It was couched in stilted, elaborate language, as if to convey some deep meaning. On analysis, it proved to say nothing at all.

Elizabeth could not stop speculation. One possible male heir was the Earl of Huntingdon. His claim went back through his mother to a brother of Edward IV. He was, at best an outsider. Among those with some traces of Tudor blood, there was Lady Catherine Grey, Lady Jane's younger sister. She was a Protestant, and a number of Members of Parliament were known to favour her strongly. It was generally felt that Elizabeth would never acknowledge her. Lady Catherine had got married in secret to a son of the late Protector Somerset. Nobody knew until it became rather obvious that she was having a baby. Elizabeth had flown into one of her rages. She said that it was treason for Catherine to get married without consulting herself, and packed her off to the Tower. In one of her less far-seeing moments, she sent Catherine's husband off to the Tower as well. When the news came out that they were having another baby, the Court held its breath in fear. Elizabeth's fury knew no bounds. She declared the children, both boys, illegitimate, so that they could not succeed to the throne. It looked as if Elizabeth was not only unwilling to marry and have children herself, but reacted quite unreasonably when anyone else did so. For the moment, those around her kept a strict watch on their tongues. It was not yet fashionable to look for explanations of people's behaviour in the events of their childhood.

With Catherine out of action, the descendants of Margaret Tudor were left. They were, by her first marriage to James IV of Scotland, Mary Queen of Scots. By her second marriage there was a grandson called Henry Stuart Lord Darnley.

For the moment, Elizabeth was more interested in Mary. If she were to marry a foreign prince, it would give another country potential power over England. If she married the imbecile Don Carlos of Spain this would mean, for all practical purposes, that Philip II once again claimed a part in English affairs. It was just possible that she might marry her own brother-in-law, the very young King of France. To Elizabeth, it was unthinkable that England should be handed over to France. She felt especially strongly since she had recently made an attempt to regain England's old possessions in France. It was to rankle as one of her worst failures.

From her experience of her own suitors, Elizabeth considered the eligible unmarried men of Europe. There was that sturdy perennial, the Archduke Charles. A young princeling called William of Orange had already been dismissed by Mary herself as too insignificant. In the end, Elizabeth decided that much the safest thing would be to have Mary marry an Englishman. That, of course, meant an Englishman whom she herself could trust. In one of the more bizarre comedies in history, Elizabeth suggested that Mary should marry Dudley.

The Scottish ambassador can be forgiven for not taking her seriously to begin with. Then the awful thought struck him that maybe she really meant it. He played for time by remarking that it was a great proof of her love for Mary that "she was willing to give her a thing so dearly prized by herself".

As it became clear that Elizabeth was in earnest, Mary had genuine grounds for feeling insulted. Dudley was the son of a proved traitor, and no woman likes to be handed another woman's cast-offs. She was provoked into renewing her schemes for a Spanish marriage. This subjected her to further harangues from John Knox. "What are you to do with my marriage?" she wailed, dabbing her streaming eyes. "Or what are you within this Commonwealth?" "A subject born within the same, Madam," retorted Knox, in his most squashing manner. Mary ran out of "napkins" with which to mop up her tears.

To make things worse for her, Philip now seemed cool about the idea of her marrying Don Carlos. It was, in fact, becoming increasingly clear that Don Carlos should not be allowed to marry at all. With some pique, she declined a suggestion that she and Elizabeth should meet. Elizabeth meanwhile turned her attention to trying to make Dudley look less like her own rejected lover. She created him Earl of Leicester, a title which had been preserved in the past for members of the royal family. When accounts of his investiture reached Mary, they did not improve her temper. In the most serious part of the ceremony, when Leicester was kneeling in homage, Elizabeth had leant forward and tickled his neck.

On a more statesman-like level, Cecil continued, in letters to Scotland, to urge the marriage. He had no great liking for Leicester, as he now was, but he was realistic enough to accept the man's existence. In any case, he was all too aware that Elizabeth's sudden death without an heir could well lead to civil war. A rule of Mary and Leicester would be better than that. Not for the first or the last time, he reflected that Elizabeth's refusal to look beyond her own death was very self-centred.

Leicester himself showed no great signs of enthusiasm. Mary might be a desirable bride, but Edinburgh was a very long way from the centre of things. It is possible that he looked round for some way out. No one had yet exploited young Henry Stuart, Lord Darnley. He was Mary's first cousin, and had some claim to succeed her as King of Scotland. In the eyes of a number of Catholics, he had a claim to the English throne which was better than Mary's, because he had been born in England.

As an English subject with claims to the throne, Darnley could not leave England without Elizabeth's permission. There was some surprise when she gave him permission to travel to Scotland. One theory was that Leicester and Cecil, in temporary alliance, had persuaded her to allow him. Another theory was that Elizabeth felt it was safer for England if Mary married Darnley than if she married a foreigner. The way things worked out has suggested a third possibility. Could it be that Elizabeth, tired of hearing of Mary's perfections, was acting out of sheer malice?

This could only be so if she knew what Darnley was really like. To look at, he was a handsome young man, and conspicuously tall. He had agreeable manners, and was moderately accomplished. When he arrived in Edinburgh, Mary said that he was "the lustiest and best-proportioned long man she had ever seen". No doubt she was glad to find a man taller than herself.

Mary had now been a widow for more than four years. She had been deprived of her happy home in France, and Elizabeth, her nearest relation, had done nothing whatever to make her feel welcome in Britain. Unlike Elizabeth, who was essentially independent, she liked to have a man on whom to lean for advice. She was in a mood to fall in love with someone, and Darnley, young and handsome, was there to hand.

So Darnley became Mary's Dudley. Like Dudley, he was vain, selfish, and boastful. But whereas Dudley had mellowed into quite a respectable citizen, Darnley, beneath the surface, was vicious and depraved. No saving instinct warned Mary of this. Her folly was greater than Elizabeth's had been, because she loved the worse man.

There was another difference between the two women.

Elizabeth behaved rashly, but in the end did nothing that would compromise her position as queen. Mary, with one single toss, threw away her best bargaining card for her right to the English throne. If she were to marry with Elizabeth's good-will, Elizabeth might give in and recognize her as successor. To marry without consulting Elizabeth, especially to marry an English subject, would give a very good pretext for Elizabeth to disown her.

This being so, Mary got married.

CHAPTER SEVEN

MARRIAGE PROBLEMS

"Cupid all arm'd: a certain aim he took
At a fair vestal throned by the west,
And loos'd his love-shaft smartly from his bow,
As it should pierce a hundred-thousand hearts:
But I might see young Cupid's fiery shaft
Quench'd in the chaste beams of the watery moon,
And the imperial vot'ress passed on,
In maiden meditation, fancy-free."

Shakespeare, *A Midsummer Night's Dream*
(thought to refer to Elizabeth).

For a short time, Mary appeared triumphant. She had married Darnley without Elizabeth's consent, which showed that she would not allow Elizabeth to be over-bearing towards her. She had someone to help her govern. She had also the normal feminine sense of superiority which any woman who has just acquired a husband feels toward a spinster.

Soon a truth began to emerge which Elizabeth may well have known all along. Whoever a queen married, some groups of her subjects were bound to object. In Scotland, where feuds between clans were an ancient tradition, the risk was especially great. The Hamilton family, who were next in line for the throne after Mary, disliked seeing Darnley's claim strengthened. Mary's illegitimate half-brother, the Protestant Earl of Moray, also disliked Darnley. He rose in rebellion. Mary acted promptly. She pledged her jewels in order to mobilize troops, and rode out at the head of her forces. The excitement went to her head like wine. She loved riding and hunting, and all through her life was to alternate long periods of ill-health with an almost frenzied craving for fresh air and exercise. She was a skilful horse-woman, and had undoubted physical courage. "Albeit the most part waxed weary, yet the Queen's courage increased manlike, so much that she was ever with the foremost." The tribute came from none other than John Knox.

Elizabeth's role was very much less romantic. She stayed in London wondering whether or not to help Moray and his rebels. In the end, she decided not to. There were strong hints that France and Spain, as well as the Pope, would support Mary if necessary. The last thing in the world Elizabeth wanted was a Catholic league. Far better to keep the Catholic powers divided with their own rivalries between themselves. The most she would do was to promise Moray asylum in England if his rebellion failed. It did, and he fled over the border. He came to London where, in the presence of two French ambassadors, Elizabeth made him kneel before her and gave him a thorough scolding. The episode was duly reported in Scotland, but not the suspicion, often since voiced, that Elizabeth and Moray had already rehearsed the whole scene.

After this one gesture, Elizabeth continued to do nothing. She smiled a little, hooded her heavy-lidded eyes, and fiddled with the ends of her elegant fingers. Everybody around her urged her to carry out a firm policy. Elizabeth smiled again. Her advisers retreated behind closed doors, and muttered to one another. The Queen, they said, as they were to say so often, was really impossible. Elizabeth still said nothing. But was there a faint watchfulness under those heavy lids? Perhaps in old age she would come to look like a bird of prey.

Life had long since taught Elizabeth that, provided one does not commit oneself, the whole nature of a situation can change. By waiting, and being patient, one may see one's opponent make some fatal mistake.

Certainly things were changing in Scotland. Reports told Elizabeth that Mary was starting to see the true nature of the man she had married. Darnley was proving selfish and avid for power. At the same time, he was unwilling to take any responsibility. He preferred to spend his days in hunting or hawking. A fierce argument was taking place as to how far he, the Queen's husband, should be looked upon as King. Unlike a modern consort, such as the Duke of Edinburgh, he had automatically been given the title. It was not enough. Darnley wished to be King in fact, as well as in name.

Elizabeth, that cold realist, must have known very well that a husband would make this demand. Her intelligence reports told her that Darnley was being petulant at any idea that he should take second place to Mary. When he had to sign documents after her, he took care to make his writing bigger. One set of coins was, indeed, issued with his name in front of Mary's, but it was soon withdrawn. This was taken to confirm reports that Mary was rapidly becoming disenchanted with him. Only one really good thing had happened from Mary's point of view: she was going to have a child. If it were a boy, he would naturally succeed to the Scottish throne and would put an end to all arguments about that. It would also mean that there was someone with strong claims to succeed to the English throne in the next generation.

Her pregnancy apart, Mary's situation was rapidly growing worse. She herself did not fully understand this. Gradually, something began to be clear about Mary, something to which the enchantment of her looks and personality had hitherto blinded a great many people. That was how confused and uncertain her judgement was.

Elizabeth seemed to have been born with a sixth sense, like an insect's antennae or the whiskers of a cat. She could feel, almost sniff, her way through the most delicate situation. Mary was entirely lacking in this gift. Nor did she seem to have much common sense to use in its place.

The first hint of what was going to happen came in Mary's choice of a new adviser. Since her return to Scotland, she had relied mainly upon two men, her brother, Moray and another Protestant, William Maitland. Maitland had been described by Elizabeth as "the flower of the wits in Scotland". He was a man with whom Cecil had had many dealings on terms of shared respect. So long as he was in charge of affairs, Scotland could carry on good diplomatic relations with England.

Then Mary ceased to trust Maitland. He was obviously unenthusiastic about her marriage. When Mary found out, in due course, that Darnley was little more than a drunken degenerate, it did not make her like Maitland any the more. Nobody likes to be proved wrong. She looked around for someone to fill the gap, for, unlike Elizabeth, she was a woman who always longed for support. Her choice of a confidant caused as much comment as if a modern queen had dismissed her Prime Minister and placed all her trust in her hairdresser instead.

David Riccio was an Italian who had come to Mary's court in the capacity of a musician. He had stayed because she wanted a bass singer to complete a quartet. He was an amusing conversationalist, and no doubt seemed a link with what Mary thought of as the more civilized world of continental Europe. The mere fact that he stood aside from the warring factions in Scotland would, in itself, have been a relief to her. He was also a Catholic, which she found sympathetic. Already, before her marriage, she had promoted him to be her French secretary.

When Darnley first came to Scotland, he and Riccio became close friends. As Mary's marriage began to break down, the whole situation changed. Darnley's behaviour was growing worse and worse. He got violently drunk, and insulted Mary in public. While his influence over Mary grew less, Riccio's became even greater.

Rumour even had it that Mary had cast her husband aside and had taken Riccio for a lover. As Elizabeth had found out long ago, such stories spread very easily. There is absolutely no evidence to support the idea. It does, however, reflect on the closeness of their relationship, and on the amount of time that Riccio spent with her. He was now the main influence in her life. As the horrified onlookers were quick to comment, neither his past experience, nor his present behaviour, gave him the remotest qualifications for such a position of trust. On Mary's part, the relationship betrayed that same lack of judgement that she had already shown in her choice of a husband.

Her association with Riccio was not allowed to continue. Darnley never a temperate man, was inflamed by jealousy, and his relations with Mary grew steadily worse. "I know now for certain that the Queen repenteth her marriage, that she hateth the King and all his kin," reported the English agent in Scotland. But Darnley did not give up hope. In a desperate bid to gain the "crown matrimonial" he made a deal with the Protestant leaders, including the exiled Moray. In return for their help in being recognized as a full king, he promised to uphold the Protestant faith in Scotland, and to return the lands they had forfeited by their recent rebellion. No mention of Riccio's position was made, but it was obvious that they could not achieve their ends unless he was ousted.

Stories of this reached London. Certainly, Cecil and Leicester knew what was afoot. Elizabeth, too, knew something, at any rate enough to realize that Mary would soon run into trouble. Not even the chequered history of her own youth can have prepared her for what actually happened.

The first act of the astonishing drama that followed was played out in the Palace of Holyroodhouse. The palace was built on to an ancient abbey, from which the monks had been driven a few years before. Bleak hills brooded above it. There, in a little room that can still be seen, Mary was sitting at supper with a few companions, among them Riccio. It was an informal occasion, for Mary was six months pregnant, and the smallness of the room, no more than twelve foot square, gave the whole setting an air of intimacy. The room was secluded, and only reached from below by a steep, twisting spiral staircase. The glow of the candles, the windows shut firmly against the night outside, gave an illusion of safety.

Suddenly Darnley burst into the room, followed by a companion, Lord Ruthven. Ruthven's appearance was strange and terrifying. He had armour showing beneath his clothes and his eyes burnt with delirium. He started to shout out a wild denunciation of Riccio. A few minutes later, a group of armed men rushed in. The supper table was knocked over, and most of the candles went out. Riccio clung to the Queen's skirts to protect himself. By such dim and flickering light as remained, he was seized and dragged loose from her, by men brandishing pistols and daggers. Mary feared for her own life, and the life of her unborn child. The men forced Riccio out of the room. The sound of his voice, screaming for mercy, became fainter and fainter. Then it stopped altogether. Later his body was found on the floor in a room below. It had over fifty stab wounds.

Once again, physical danger brought out the best in Mary. When told of Riccio's death, she is said to have remarked, "No tears now; I will think upon revenge." Her scheme to break up the alliance between Darnley and his fellow conspirators was simple, and, for the moment, very effective. Using her knowledge of Darnley's weak character, she persuaded him to escape from Holyroodhouse with her before any further violence could be done. With their figurehead gone, the group of conspirators fled. The exiled Moray returned to Scotland and made his peace with her.

For the moment, Mary's star seemed again to be in the ascendant. In this state, she did what was expected of every queen. In June 1566, she produced a son. This, above all, was the moment in their lives when she outshone Elizabeth. Many years later, the story was told that, when Elizabeth heard the news, she burst out, "The Queen of Scots is lighter of a fair son, and I am but a barren stock!"

Whatever the truth of this story, the mere existence of young James Stuart made the question of Elizabeth's own marriage more urgent. The likeliest, or it might be more accurate to say the least unlikely candidate, was the Archduke Charles of Austria. He combined the advantage of belonging to a royal family with the equally great advantage of being a younger son. If Elizabeth married him, England would not become subordinate to another country. The great problem was Elizabeth herself.

Once again she was insisting, against all precedent for royal ladies, of having some first-hand knowledge of her possible bridegroom. It was thought she might send spies to report on him, and everyone knew that Elizabeth liked lively, high-spirited men. So Charles was decked out in new clothes, and mounted on "fiery steeds" instead of his usual "hacks or palfreys". A great deal was made of the question as to whether or not the Archduke was a little deformed. As there were then no photographs, it was hard to tell, so Cecil took anxious notes about hints on a "neck bent towards the left side" and "a very little round-shouldered". Elizabeth suggested that he should steal over to England in disguise so that she could see for herself.

It was impossible not to suspect that she was enjoying the whole situation. Meanwhile, her advisers were busy negotiating about the crucial problem of the Archduke's religion. One of the major achievements of Elizabeth's first years on the throne had been to establish a compromise in the Church of England. The historical form of church organization, with bishops, had been kept, while, to satisfy the reformers, church services were to be based on the Protestant Prayer Book of 1552. This settlement did not suit extremists on either side, but it did accommodate the maximum number of moderate men in the middle. The advantages to the country were too great to be thrown away, even for the sake of getting Elizabeth married. The English therefore insisted that the Archduke should attend Anglican services in public, although he might hear Mass in private. The Emperor, on behalf of his son, demanded a public place for Charles's Catholic worship.

As the weary negotiations dragged on, Cecil tried hard to persuade himself that it was all worth-while. He wrote down two lists in parallel columns, a method of clearing his mind of which he was very fond. Under the headings of the Archduke and Leicester, he wrote down the advantages to be gained from marriage with either. Birth, reputation, wealth, the benefit to England: in every category the advantage was on the Archduke's side. Leicester, he wrote austerely, "shall study nothing but to enhance his own particular friends to wealth, to office, to lands, and to offend others". He turned to brood on the further demand that Charles must be crowned King of England.

Elizabeth, too, heard this, and maybe she thought of Darnley. As if to confuse the issue, so far as everyone else was concerned, she sent for reports on the rival charms of the King of France. He was then a ripe fourteen. She also indulged in a wild flirtation with a married courtier called Thomas Heneage. The House of Commons deplored her frivolity, and decided to make her take matters more seriously.

Parliament under Elizabeth had not yet acquired the importance that it had with her successors. It had already shown that it had a mind of its own. Its power over the sovereign was based on the vital fact that it voted money. After the birth of James Stuart, Elizabeth realized that unless she would either name her successor or give a firm promise to marry, Parliament might well withhold her supplies. The House of Lords seemed prepared to join with the House of Commons. Elizabeth was furious. At Court, she raged and stormed at her nobles. All the discreditable stories that she knew about them, and she knew a surprising number, were flung in their faces. The Commons retorted by passing the minimum number of bills. The subsidy bill, granting Elizabeth money, was carefully left at its first reading stage. It was decided that Parliament should petition the Queen, and ask her to make her mind up about the succession.

Before they could act, the Queen summoned a deputation of Lords and Commons to come before her. Then, with her usual lack of inhibition, she really let fly at them.

Why, she demanded, should they attack her? "Was I not born in the realm? Were my parents born in any foreign country? ... Is not my kingdom here? Whom have I oppressed? Whom have I enriched to other's harm? ... How have I governed since my reign?"

She then declared her intention to marry. "I did send them answer that I would marry, although of mine own disposition I was not inclined thereunto.... And I hope to have children, otherwise I would never marry." It was strange, she added crushingly, that they would not believe their sovereign's word when it was spoken.

She went on to the succession question, and pointed out, from her own experience, how many plots could be woven around the successor to a throne. It was dangerous to the heir as well as to the ruler. She herself had suffered in plots against her sister. She implied that they were meddling in matters which concerned herself more closely than them. "Nothing was said for my safety, but only for themselves. A strange thing that the foot should direct the head in so weighty a cause."

Finally, she reminded them of her own powers, both in terms of the constitution and as an individual person. "And though I be a woman, yet have I as good a courage, answerable to my place, as ever my father had. I am your annointed Queen. I will never be by violence constrained to do anything. I thank God I am endued with such qualities that if I were turned out of the realm in my petticoat, I were able to live in any place in Christendom."

It was a picturesque thought, and no one who knew Elizabeth could doubt it was true. There had seldom been a woman more capable of looking after herself in any circumstances. It did not affect Parliament's view on the main issue which was that she ought to decide about the succession. In the end, she had to withdraw her claim to one-third of the money she wanted, in order to get them in a good temper again. The marriage situation did not sort itself out, for the Archduke would not come to England. Elizabeth refused to make any concessions about religion unless she could see for herself what sort of a bargain she was getting. When Parliament rose at the beginning of January 1567, the question of marriage and the succession was still as undecided as ever.

In just over a month, the whole situation had changed, in an almost unbelievable way.

CHAPTER EIGHT

TREACHEROUS GROUND

"Scotland is a quagmire."

William Cecil in April 1567.

With the birth of James, Mary was in a strong position. She was mother of a child who might become the first person to unite the English and Scottish crowns. Elizabeth had made the gesture of standing god-mother to him. There was also some hope of peace in Scotland, for Mary had become reconciled to Maitland and the other Protestant lords. Two things marred her future. One was her own intermittent bouts of ill-health when, so far as can be told four hundred years later, she suffered from both violent stomach pains and hysterical nervous symptoms. The other problem was the existence of Darnley.

Darnley was proving quite intolerable. He was a mixture of weakness and attempted tyranny, of pretensions to the throne and violent dissipation. Neither as a queen nor as a woman could Mary feel any respect or affection for him. Elizabeth's envoy, the Earl of Bedford, reported that the situation between them was "rather worse. She eateth but very seldom with him... but keepeth no company with him, nor loveth any such as love him... It cannot for modesty nor the honour of a Queen be reported what she said of him."

Then even the attractive appearance, which had drawn Mary to Darnley originally, suddenly disappeared. He was stricken with some unpleasant, spotty disease, and had to keep his face hidden behind a taffeta mask. What had caused it is not now certain, but he had become, at best, an object of pity.

In this condition, Mary brought him to Edinburgh. From here begins one of the strangest and most disputed episodes in British history. It is fairly clear what happened, but how it happened and why it happened has been argued about ever since.

Mary did not take Darnley to Holyroodhouse, but to a much smaller place called Kirk o' Field. The site is now part of Edinburgh University. While he was there, she spent a fair amount of time with him, and normally slept in the house in a room below his own. Then at ten or eleven one evening, she suddenly decided to go to Holyroodhouse to be present at the wedding masque of one of her attendants. This meant that she was away for the rest of the night.

Nobody can tell now what Mary intended. Those who admire her character as a romantic queen, see nothing in this situation except wifely concern. It is argued that she chose Kirk o' Field as a suitable place for a convalescent. The time that she spent with Darnley, in contrast to her recent avoidance of him, is seen as a final attempt to restore good relations with him.

On the other hand, there are those who look upon Mary Queen of Scots as a sketch for Shakespeare's Lady Macbeth. If this is so, she had brought Darnley to Kirk o' Field as part of a cunning and deliberate plot. There remains a third possibility: that Mary had some awareness of what was happening but lacked either the will or the ability to take control of events.

For what happened was a dramatic as anything out of *Macbeth*. Mary went off to dance at Holyroodhouse. Some time, perhaps during the night after she had left, some men stole into Kirk o' Field and laid a trail of gunpowder. In the darkness and cold of the early hours of the February morning, the people of Edinburgh were woken by a violent explosion. When it became light enough to see what had happened, it was found that Kirk o' Field had been wrecked completely. Surprisingly, Darnley's body was found not inside the house, but in the garden outside. He was dressed only in his night clothes, as if he had found something to warn him of danger and had tried to escape. But somebody had been lying in wait for him. He had been strangled.

Had Darnley died naturally, his loss would have been a fortunate thing for Mary. As it was, the scandal of the explosion echoed throughout Scotland and far beyond. Nearly everyone made the same comment: that Mary stood to gain by her husband's death. Her whole future as Queen was threatened.

It was in this situation that Elizabeth wrote to Mary. Her letter contained no sign that she was a woman who herself had been tainted by scandal when Amy Robsart had died. Instead, she wrote in the tones of an outraged queen. She did not address Mary as a dear sister, in her usual manner, but began tersely, "Madam".

"My ears have been so astounded," she wrote, "and my heart so frightened to hear of the horrible and abominable murder of your husband and my own cousin that I have scarcely spirit to write: yet I cannot conceal that I grieve more for you than for him. I should not do the office of a faithful cousin and friend, if I did not urge you to preserve your honour."

There spoke an adept in the art of political survival. Mary's immediate care ought to be for her reputation. What she needed above all was to prove herself innocent of her husband's death. This could best be done by disassociating herself from the Protestant lords who were suspected of causing it; "those who have done you that pleasure as most people say", in Elizabeth's words.

Foremost among the suspects was a man called Lord Bothwell.

It was not long before rumours about Bothwell reached England and France. The common people of Edinburgh had no doubt in their minds as to who was guilty of Darnley's murder. Placards appeared on the streets. Because many people could not read, they took the form of pictures. One showed Bothwell as a hare, his family crest, crouched in a circle of swords. Mary was shown above him, with the initials M. R., as a naked mermaid. Their two names became inextricably linked in most people's minds.

Mary would not act against Bothwell. It was Darnley's father who started a private action to try to prove him guilty of murder. The trial was a farce. Edinburgh was packed with the armed supporters of Bothwell, and Darnley's father did not dare to appear. In the absence of an accuser, Bothwell was acquitted without any evidence being considered. He went away swaggering through the streets. This did nothing to improve public opinion, which still suspected that Mary was guilty and had lured Darnley to his death. The only way she could regain her reputation would have been by an outright condemnation of Bothwell. Instead, she made it disastrously clear that Bothwell was the one person in whom she trusted.

Mary wanted someone to lean on. So far, neither her weak and depraved husband, Darnley, nor the turbulent Scottish lords, had proved a reliable prop. In Bothwell she imagined that she had at last found somebody with whom she could share her troubles. He was an ugly and vigorous man of tremendously strong personality. Her trust in him may simply have been a part of that sheer lack of common sense that she had shown already in marrying Darnley and in choosing Riccio as an adviser. Did she never stop to think what her subjects would say when she associated with a man who was suspected of murdering her own husband? In fact, what her subjects had to say was extremely simple. Bothwell was notorious for getting his own way with women. Most people assumed that Mary was wildly in love with him.

Only very quick wits and a great deal of wiliness could have got her out of the trouble that she was now in. Elizabeth, in the same situation, might have managed to save herself. Mary was either quite happy with things as they were, or else she was prepared to let events overwhelm her. The next startling twist in her story came two months after Darnley's death, when she had been to Stirling where her ten-month old son was staying. She was riding back to Edinburgh with a small escort when Bothwell intercepted her and demanded that she go with him. She offered so little resistance, that many people had the impression the whole thing was pre-arranged. What Mary herself hoped to gain is impossible to tell. In Bothwell's case, it was a decisive move in a scheme to marry her and obtain supreme power in Scotland.

In point of fact, Bothwell was already married, but he was not the type of man to let that stand in his way. His wife agreed to divorce him on the grounds of adultery. The woman involved was called Bessie Crawford, but she could have been one of many others. Mary's detractors were quick to point out that she could have been Mary.

Three months after her husband's death, Mary and Bothwell were married. No special wedding clothes were ordered; and Mary loved clothes; and hardly any gifts given. The ceremony was a simple Protestant one. That Mary, the champion of Catholicism, should have agreed to a Protestant ceremony was surprising. Either she was completely dominated by Bothwell or else she had passed into an almost trance-like state in which she no longer cared what happened to her.

All this time, Elizabeth had waited, while the violent logic of events took its course. She was fond of allowing other people to wear themselves out by their own struggles before she acted. This did not take long to happen. Any hopes Mary had entertained that the Protestant nobles would accept Bothwell as overlord, proved to be entirely mistaken. Bothwell had made himself hated by his ambition and self-seeking. Rather than accept him in power, the Protestant lords rose against him and Mary. The two were beseiged in Borthwick Castle, near Edinburgh. They escaped one at a time, with Mary disguised as a man. For the next few weeks she was hounded through Scotland, but would not abandon Bothwell. Then a month after their marriage, he managed to escape, and finally went abroad. Mary surrendered herself to the lords. She was driven to Edinburgh, where, for the first time, she became fully aware of how the common people of Scotland felt about her and about Darnley's murder. "Burn her, burn her, she is not worthy to live," they shouted when she appeared. As she rode on in her mud-stained clothes, they pressed closer to her, crying out, "Kill her, drown her." The men were bitter about her, but the women, report said, were worse.

Mary was imprisoned on an island in Loch Leven. The castle can still be seen, raised not very much above the level of dark, brooding waters. In Mary's time, the island on which it stood is thought to have been even smaller than it is now. There, in that bleak and dismal setting, Mary miscarried of twins.

It now looked as if this extraordinary train of events was over. Elizabeth was at last willing to act. She could see that Mary's imprisonment meant an absence of any clear power in Scotland. The question of who controlled the baby prince James would be of increasing importance. She did not want the gap to be filled by France.

The best solution, from Elizabeth's point of view, would have been to restore Mary herself to the throne. Elizabeth was a true daughter of the sixteenth century, and like most of her contemporaries believed very strongly in an ordered form of society. She thought that those born to high office had a God-given right to exercise power, and her own future depended upon her subjects believing this too. Whatever happened, she did not want the infection of civil disorder to spread from England to Scotland. She therefore sent an envoy, Sir Nicholas Throgmorton, to Scotland. His task was to urge that Mary should not be imprisoned by those "that by nature and law are subjected to her".

At the same time, Elizabeth knew very well that a ruler needed to win the good-will of those whom he governed. Much of her own success was because of the way she had always set out to win people's affections. In marrying Bothwell, Mary had cast this idea to the wind. A few weeks before, Elizabeth had written to Mary pointing out her mistake. "How could a worse choice be made for your honour than in such haste to marry a subject who, beside other notorious lacks, public fame has charged with the murder of your late husband? . . . And with what peril have you married him, that hath another lawful wife alive?" continued the daughter of Henry VIII. Now that Mary was imprisoned, she suggested to the Scottish lords that one condition of freeing her should be a divorce from Bothwell. Once again, she urged Mary herself to take action against the murderers of her husband.

Elizabeth's efforts to turn the clock back got nowhere. Throgmorton was not even allowed to see Mary in her island fortress in Loch Leven. The Scottish lords forced her to abdicate. In July 1567, the thirteen-month-old James Stuart was crowned King of Scotland in a church just outside Stirling Castle. The baby who had been baptized as a Catholic only the year before became the first Protestant King of Scotland. Moray returned from England to act as regent for his young nephew.

Elizabeth made threatening noises. She worked up a great deal of passion, and subjected Cecil to what he called "a great offensive speech" about the Scottish lords. To his alarm, she insisted on sending a letter demanding Mary's freedom. He bewailed the fact that she might have lost him "the fruits of seven or eight years negotiations with Scotland, and now to suffer a divorce between this realm and that".

The Scots lords simply ignored her. Maitland told Throgmorton that, if she wished to make war, "We had rather endure the misfortune thereof and suffer the sequel than put the Queen to liberty now in this mood that she is in." At the end of August, Throgmorton returned to London, having accomplished nothing.

Elizabeth was now faced with a difficult choice. Should she carry out her threats to free Mary, or should she recognize Moray as regent? Then civil war broke out again in France. This made the whole affair less urgent, for the French were too busy to interfere in Scotland. Elizabeth was able to take the sort of compromise course that was natural to her. She declined to accept an ambassador from Moray, because that would have recognized his right to govern Scotland. She did, however, let Cecil carry on quite a friendly correspondence with him, in which the title of regent was never actually used. Moray was somewhat amused by the whole matter. He had got Elizabeth's measure.

There was one question, at least, in which Elizabeth had proved wiser than anybody around her. Cecil, her Council, and Parliament had all repeatedly urged her to marry. On Cecil's part at least, this showed a genuine lack of self-interest. The mere existence of a husband for Elizabeth would, inevitably, have weakened his own position. But he was concerned, above all, to secure an heir to the throne.

Elizabeth saw more clearly. There seems no doubt

that she was reluctant to commit herself to any lasting human relationship. She had an emotional nervousness, probably the result of her childhood and adolesence, which is not an attractive or a generous feature. But beyond this, she had a deep political wisdom. It was far better for a queen to remain unmarried than to make a mistake in marrying which could divide her kingdom. It was true that by marrying, she might produce an heir. Was a baby worth possible civil war? He would be unable to rule for at least twenty years, and Edward's reign had showed clearly the problems of having a child as king. If any thing could show the dangers of a queen's marrying it was surely the disastrous story of Mary.

Then, the following year, in May 1568, events took yet another twist. With a mixture of daring and ingenuity, Mary got hold of a boat and escaped from Loch Leven Castle. She raised a small army, but it was defeated and she had to flee. "I have had to sleep upon the ground," she wrote to an uncle in France, "and drink sour milk, and eat oatmeal without bread, and have been three nights like the owls."

She knew she could not stay in Scotland. Her supporters urged her to go to France. The rulers were friendly to her, and she still had the wealth and estates of a dowager queen of the country. She could have reached France safely by taking the westerly route past Wales and Cornwall, the same route that she had taken as a small child. It was the obvious and sensible thing to do, but Mary had a gift for surprising, extravagant gestures. She crossed over the Solway Firth, and landed in England.

CHAPTER NINE

THE UNWELCOME GUEST

"Two stars keep not their motion in one sphere;
Nor can one England brook a double reign."
Shakespeare, *King Henry IV Part I*.

Elizabeth did not want her. The truth was as simple as that. What on earth was she supposed to do with the woman? She could send her back to France, where Ronsard could write a few more immortal poems to her. But the last time Mary had been in France, she had laid open claims to be Queen of England. Alternatively, she could bring her to court in London. Here too, Mary might set up as a rival. In any case, did Elizabeth really want her, with her gift for alluring men and her extraordinary capacity for having disastrous incidents take place around her? The best thing would be to put her out of action. Elizabeth's own instinct was to send her back to be Queen of Scotland, where she belonged. Cecil and most of the Privy Council would have preferred to keep her under restraint in England. In the background of everyone's mind lurked the thought that one way of making Mary harmless would be to put her out of the way—for ever.

From that moment, the key to Mary's future lay in Elizabeth's hands. No one can tell what Elizabeth really thought of Mary, for on this, as on all other vital issues, she kept her own inner silence. She clearly found Mary annoying at times, as a school-mistress finds a pupil who is at the same time backwards and lamentably precocious.

Yet she could not fail to be conscious, as Mary was herself, that they were closer in circumstance to one another than to any other living person. Mary, the woman who happened to be a monarch, was the distorted mirror-image of Elizabeth, the monarch who happened to be a woman. They were bound together, whether they liked it or not. In a world where the mere existence of a woman as sovereign was precarious and suspected, Elizabeth knew that to injure Mary might be to injure herself. So began the strange situation in which the chief defender of Mary's life was Elizabeth. By all masculine logic, nobody stood to gain more by Mary's death.

Already Elizabeth, by keeping silent, had saved Mary's life. With a little encouragement from her, the Scottish lords would have executed Mary before she escaped from Loch Leven. When Mary arrived in England, Elizabeth wished, against her Council's advice, to welcome her as a fellow queen. For the moment, the problem was solved by keeping Mary at Carlisle, near the Scottish border, in a state which was not close captivity but was certainly not freedom either.

Elizabeth's Councillors saw very clearly that Mary's mere existence as a rival to the throne was a threat to Elizabeth's life. This did not weigh with Elizabeth. It was one of the many contradictions of her character that she, the most ultra-cautious of politicians, was downright rash about her own personal safety. This quality of obvious physical courage was one of the things which helped her to make such a deep impact when she appeared in public. It terrified her advisers.

The other great problem about Mary was that she was a woman implicated in the murder of her own husband. Since women were thought of as being subject to men, this was a graver offence than a man's being involved in murdering his own wife. Elizabeth's advisers decided to try to establish the question of Mary's guilt. There is no doubt that they hoped she would be found guilty, because this would provide a pretext for keeping Mary under restraint.

So an enquiry into Mary's affairs was opened. Mary agreed to it. With an optimism that she was to transmit to some of her ill-starred descendants, she hoped it would clear her name, and that Elizabeth would then restore her to the Scottish throne. It might have been thought that nothing else melodramatic could happen, for a few weeks at any rate. This was to underestimate Mary's magnetic gift for attracting trouble. Soon, the new topic of scandal was what are known as the Casket Letters.

The letters are so called because they were found in a casket. From the first, there was a mystery about them. The official story was that they were taken from one of Bothwell's retainers at the time when he fled and Mary surrendered. According to this version, Moray made use of the letters to secure Mary's abdication. Since then, a number of people have pointed out that there is no definite evidence that the letters were known at that time. Did they just appear, very conveniently, at a point when Elizabeth seemed over-sympathetic to Mary?

The contents of the casket were some poems, two marriage contracts, and a number of letters. The letters are written as from a woman, whose name is not given, to an unknown man. The longest letter is often rambling and incoherent, as if written under the stress of a strong emotion. It speaks of her love for the man to whom she was writing, and attacks her husband as somebody loathsome to her. She says, however, that she will pretend to act in a friendly way to him, in order to get him to move from his present dwelling. The parallel with Mary's situation was obvious. The letters were taken as proof that Mary had been in love with Bothwell before Darnley's death, and that she had lured him to Kirk o' Field in order that he could be killed.

It is impossible now to tell whether that was true. The originals of the letters have disappeared. Some exist in contemporary copies, others only in translation so that nobody knows for certain what the originals said. Much the most satisfactory thing would be to have the letters examined by a modern handwriting expert. Unless the originals ever turn up, this cannot be done.

At the time, the letters made a great impression, and were taken as proof that Mary had played a part in the murder. The enquiry petered out, without reaching any official conclusion, and Mary was taken back to what could, at best, be called house-arrest.

Does this mean that Mary's future was changed by evidence against her which may quite well have been forged? The answer is probably not. The Casket Letters make a picturesque story, like so much else about Mary, but in the end they are irrelevant. There were already plenty of people who thought her guilty of Darnley's murder. Their case did not depend on the Casket Letters, but on the whole pattern of her behaviour at the time of his death. Besides, there were too many other factors at work for the English to let Mary go free. The views of Cecil and other advisers came to triumph over Elizabeth's own more tolerant ones. She, like Mary, was to be at the mercy of events.

Beneath all her vanities and her posturings, her intellectual tortuousnesses, the basic fact about Elizabeth was that she loved peace and order. Nowhere was this more true than in her attitude to religion. When she had come to the throne she had helped establish a national church designed to attract the greatest possible number of people. It had reformed ancient abuses, but it also avoided what the Prayer Book called "new-fangled" ideas.

For the first ten years of Elizabeth's reign, there was an atmosphere of religious calm in England. This was an amazing achievement. During the previous reign, her sister had executed over three hundred people in five years for their religious views. In France, a whole series of religious wars was taking place. In Spain and the Netherlands, Catholics were persecuting Protestants. In Geneva and Scotland, the Protestants were proving that the Catholics had no monopoly of intolerance. Against this background of hatred and passion, Elizabeth asked for nothing more than civil obedience and outward conformity to the church. In a memorable phrase she said, she would "open no windows into men's souls". Her own idea of religion seems to have been that there was "only one Christ Jesus and one faith: the rest is all dispute about trifles".

This may seem true enough nowadays, but Elizabeth was speaking at a time of intense bitterness. The shock of the Reformation had now produced the Counter-Reformation, by which the Roman Catholic Church had hardened its traditional views. It had re-established the Inquisition to keep its own house in order. A remarkable man called Ignatius Loyola had founded a sort of spiritual guerilla movement known as the Jesuits. However much Elizabeth might want to keep religion a private affair, it was very much a public one.

The English attitude towards Mary was influenced by this growing religious conflict. It was also affected by diplomatic changes, notably an increasing coolness with Spain. Since Elizabeth had come to the throne, it had suited both countries to keep on good terms with each other. Signs of trouble came in their attitude to one another's ambassadors. Elizabeth made an odd choice of an ambassador to Madrid. She, who disapproved of married clergy, sent a married clergyman as ambassador to a country where all the clergy were celibate. Philip expelled him for his religious opinions. He then withdrew the Spanish ambassador in London, a man who had done much to keep good relations between the two countries,

and appointed instead a man who had no sympathy
with the English.

Then came the first real trouble. In December 1568,
Spanish ships took refuge from storms and French raiders
in the small port of Plymouth in Devon. The leading merchant in Plymouth, one William Hawkins, was interested
to know what they had on board. He decided that it was
money to pay Spanish troops in the Netherlands. Philip
had ruled the Netherlands for the last thirteen years,
ever since his father, the Emperor Charles V, had abdi-
cated and split up his vast territories. Philip was having a
great deal of trouble in keeping his Netherlands subjects
quiet, particularly the Protestant ones.

Hawkins' own sympathies were pro-Protestant and anti-
Spanish. He therefore wrote to Cecil suggesting the money
be confiscated. Cecil would not go so far as this, but
when it was found that the money still belonged to
Italian bankers, he arranged that England should borrow
the money instead of Spain. To retaliate, the Spaniards
seized English property in the Netherlands. The next
move was that the English took over Spanish possessions
in England. Of the two, they gained more in the process.
For a time, it looked as if war could break out.

Soon there was more trouble, out in the remote West
Indies. A hundred-odd Devon men sailed home half-
starved, swearing angrily and muttering eternal hatred
of Spain. The leader was Hawkins' young brother, John,
and the one other captain involved was an unknown
kinsman of theirs by the name of Drake. Officials in
London and Madrid dismissed the Devonshire seamen
as not being very important. The storm centre of the
trouble between England and Spain was now Mary
Queen of Scots.

Early in 1569, Mary told the Spanish ambassador's
servant, "Tell the ambassador that if his master will
help me, I shall be Queen of England in three months

and Mass shall be said all over the country." While the ambassador could not promise physical help, in the shape of armed forces, he was fully prepared to play his part in plots and intrigues.

The main scheme was to marry Mary to the Duke of Norfolk. He was the only duke in England and was related to Elizabeth through her mother. The marriage would have made Mary a still more powerful contender for the throne. Norfolk himself pretended not to be interested. Having read the Casket Letters he called Mary "a notorious adulterer and murderer" and commented to Elizabeth, "I love to sleep upon a safe pillow."

Linked with this was a plot to get rid of Cecil and the other "new men" and to restore the power of the old nobility. It came to nothing, largely through Elizabeth's own loyalty to Cecil. Then, in the summer of 1569, Elizabeth discovered that, in spite of all his denials, Norfolk was still actively plotting to marry Mary. Elizabeth felt she must stop him. Mary, married to the noblest lord in England, would be too great a focus for discontent. Events seemed to be reaching a climax. The Duke fled to his estates in Norfolk, and his supporters gathered round him. De Spes, the Spanish ambassador, told him that nothing could ruin his hopes, except his own cowardice. He was right. In a battle of wills, Norfolk gave in to Elizabeth. She judged he was safer out of the way, and sent him to the Tower.

Cecil suggested that the safest thing to do with Norfolk would be to marry him to somebody else. He stressed to her that "The Queen of Scots always is and always shall be a dangerous person to your estate." Once again, he urged her to marry herself.

The peaceful atmosphere, which had marked the first ten years of Elizabeth's reign, was now thoroughly disturbed. Then came a real threat of civil war, that nightmare that lurked at the back of everyone's mind. The bells of Northumberland were rung backwards, to summon men to a rising. From this wild and remote part of England there came a force of men like something out of the Middle Ages. Their leaders bore the great feudal names of the north that were famed in the Border ballads: Percy, Neville, and Dacres. They marched beneath banners that showed the five wounds of Christ. When they reached Durham Cathedral, they tore up the English Bible and Prayer Book, and celebrated Mass.

It was a neglected part of the country protesting against government from far-away London. It was the ancient nobility seeing themselves thrust aside by upstarts like Cecil. It was hill-farmers and dalesmen who longed for the old ways their fathers had known, and who feared a world that seemed to be changing too quickly. It was also an attempt to release Mary Queen of Scots, with, behind it, the threat of foreign intervention if they were successful.

The danger was great enough to rouse Elizabeth into doing two of the things that she most disliked: acting decisively and spending money. While the rest of England remained firmly behind her, she sent forces powerful enough to crush the rebels. She then punished them severely as disturbers of law and order. On the religious issue, she kept firmly to her old attitude. All she required was outward conformity to a church that was broadly based on the scriptures and on the historic creeds. "We never had any meaning or intention that our subjects should be troubled or molested by examination or inquisition in any matter, either of their faith . . . or for matter of ceremonies." This might not be religious toleration of the most heroic kind, but, among her contemporaries, only the French philosopher, Montaigne, and the Dutch Prince, William of Orange, were to take tolerance further than she did.

Soon she was to have her back to the wall. The next

person to challenge her was the Pope. Pius V was a man of great personal sanctity, who lived a life of prayer and contemplation. He had very little contact with the events of the world around him. Without consulting the Catholic rulers of Europe, he decided to take action. He declared Elizabeth, "the pretended Queen of England and servant of crime" guilty of heresy, and excommunicated her.

This, in itself, might not have worried Elizabeth greatly. Unfortunately, as the English realized when the news reached them some three months later, the Papal Bull had a nasty sting in its tail. The Pope "charged and commanded" Elizabeth's subjects that "they do not dare to obey her orders, mandates, and laws. Those who shall act to the contrary we include in the like sentence of excommunication." In other words, Elizabeth's Catholic subjects were told not to obey her civil authority. The Bull said, in effect, "Do not render unto Caesar the things that are Caesar's."

The tragic effects of the Bull upon English Catholics was not fully seen at once. Elizabeth remained calm under the provocation. She declared once again that all she asked of her subjects was that they should not "wilfully and manifestly" break the laws of the country. She said nobody could examine their consciences except for "Almighty God who is the only searcher of hearts." Elizabeth stood alone. As so very often happens, extremism of one sort promoted extremism of another.

Until the Bull, the religious situation during Elizabeth's reign had been remarkably peaceful by sixteenth-century standards. Everyone had to go to church, or pay a fine of a shilling, one twentieth of a pound. At that stage some men, such as seamen, earned only four pounds a year. Very often, the fine was not enforced, on the grounds that churchwardens "would rather commit perjury than give their neighbours cause for offence". But while

Catholics had been asked to attend church, they had not been asked to take Holy Communion. This service is the central one of the Christian religion. It is therefore a symbolic act of profound importance. To take Communion is to become a full member of a church, and to accept that church's claims. The House of Commons now proposed that taking Communion should be made compulsory by law. The cost of not doing so would be a crippling fine.

Cecil seems to have approved. So did the Privy Council. So did the House of Lords, including the bishops. All the Bill needed was for Elizabeth to consent. She refused to do so. She would not accept laws that struck at men's innermost consciences. Three more times during her reign, she used her personal powers to block similar Bills. For constancy in clinging to her ideas of tolerance, it was a personal triumph. In so far as it made the Commons more fiercely Protestant and separated them from the monarchy, it held the seeds of trouble.

There was no doubt in most people's minds that Catholics and treason were now connected. In the summer of 1570, the Duke of Norfolk was released from the Tower. He signed solemn undertakings to have no more dealings with Mary. In fact, he had got her approval before he signed. He then became involved in a plot with a Florentine banker called Ridolphi and the Spanish ambassador. The scheme was to get rid of Elizabeth with the help of Spanish forces brought in from the Netherlands. Mary would be proclaimed Queen in her place. The Pope was delighted to hear of the scheme, and wrote to Mary that he would take her and her supporters under his wings as a hen does its chickens.

It was an age of plotting and spies. Luckily for Elizabeth, Cecil, just created Lord Burghley, had spies of his own. One of them captured letters which revealed a plot, but not the identity of two noblemen referred to as "30" and

"40". Then he had a tip-off from a merchant who was suspicious about a heavy bag which he had been asked to convey to Norfolk's agent in the north of England. It was found to contain £600. Further inquiries showed that this was money sent from the French ambassador to Mary's supporters in Scotland. One of Norfolk's houses was searched, and letters in cipher found hidden under the tiles. These revealed the whole plot. The Spanish Ambassador, who was shown to be deeply involved, was sent packing. Norfolk was brought before his fellow peers to be tried for treason.

It was the first major treason trial in fourteen years of a remarkably merciful reign. On January 16th 1572, Norfolk was found guilty and was condemned to death. He was due to be executed on the 21st, but Elizabeth deferred it. "The Queen's majesty hath always been a merciful lady," commented Burghley. His admiration was strongly tinged with annoyance, and also with fear. "By mercy she hath taken more harm than by justice." For the next few months, Elizabeth kept on hesitating. Once she went so far as to sign the death warrant, and then countermanded it. She had once been very close to dying a traitor's death herself. Was she able to enter, all too vividly, into the feelings of others?

In the meantime, the whole weight of Parliament was brought upon Elizabeth to urge her to execute not merely Norfolk but Mary. The Bishops quoted the Bible at her to show that it was her duty. The Privy Council implored her to put her own safety first. John Knox had already thundered away to Cecil. "If ye strike not at the root, the branches that appear to be broken will bud again, and that more quickly than men can believe.... Yours to command in God, John Knox with his one foot in the grave."

Elizabeth would not listen. It was obvious by now that any hopes that Mary in prison would be harmlessly out of the way had very little foundation. But however dangerous she might appear, Elizabeth refused to execute her. For a monarch so to hold out against her loyal advisers, who were inspired by a wish for her safety, required great strength of purpose. For a lone woman to do so, in a world dominated by men, required at least equal firmness.

She could not hold out entirely. On June 2nd 1572, Norfolk went to the scaffold. He had never seen Mary Queen of Scots, on whose behalf he was dying. On the same day, Parliament gave a second reading to a new Bill against Mary. They were deeply concerned at Elizabeth's refusal to protect herself. They said she was "lulled asleep and wrapped in the mantle of her own peril". The new Bill said that Mary's life would be forfeit if ever she sought the throne. The Bill also said that it would be treason to support Mary, "the monstrous and huge dragon and mass of the earth", as one Member called her.

Four weeks later, the Bill was presented to Elizabeth. She refused to sign it, and only said that she would consider it later. "I cannot write patiently," exclaimed Burghley, describing the episode. He went on to say that the Queen was her own worst enemy. Certainly, she was taking a serious risk. By the general standards of her day, her lack of vindictiveness was astonishing.

It was part of the deep paradox of her character. As a woman, Elizabeth was not often kind or affectionate. She had a sort of emotional withdrawal, a refusal to give herself fully. Many people have called her cold, and have been far more attracted by the extravagant follies of Mary Queen of Scots. As a ruler, she showed great mercy.

In the same way, Elizabeth was volatile and inconstant in small things. She maddened her ministers by her endless changes of mind. On more fundamental issues, such as religious tolerance and the future of Mary, she seemed to be unwavering.

Could she, almost alone, with no single person who fully shared her position, maintain her middle way? It would be increasingly hard. Less than two months after Parliament was prorogued, frightening news reached England. Had a great war between Catholics and Protestants, a fight to the bitter finish, begun at last?

CHAPTER TEN

NEW HORIZONS

"Which of the kings of this land before her Majesty, had their banners ever seen in the Caspian sea? which of them hath ever dealt with the Emperor of Persia, as her Majesty hath done? . . . what English ships did heretofore ever anchor in the mighty river of Plate? pass and repass the unpassable (in former opinion) strait of Magellan, range along the coast of Chile, Peru . . . further than any Christian ever passed, traverse the mighty breadth of the South sea . . . as the subjects of this now flourishing monarchy have done?"

Richard Hakluyt,
The Principle Navigations of the English Nation.

The news was of a massacre in France: of the Paris gutters running with blood and the River Seine flowing red. Men had been butchered like animals in hundreds, or was it in thousands? There was no telephone, radio or newspapers to bring reliable news to England. Instead, rumour swelled and grew of a massive plot to exterminate Protestantism.

The truth, when it came, was frightening. It had begun as a plot by the Queen Mother of France to assassinate the leader of the French Protestants, or Huguenots. This had been increased to a plot to kill all Huguenot leaders. At dawn on St Bartholomew's Day, August 24th 1572, the bells of one of the Paris churches rang out as a signal.

Then madness broke loose. The mainly Catholic population of Paris turned on their neighbours. They seized men, women, and children; hurled them out of windows and off roof-tops; hanged them or stabbed them to death. So far as can be discovered, four thousand were killed in Paris and as many elsewhere in France.

To the Catholic world, it was a triumph. The Pope had a medal struck in commemoration, and ordered Rome to be illuminated for three nights. Philip of Spain declared that the massacre "has given me one of the greatest joys of my life". In contrast, the Czar of Russia was shocked, and wrote to the French to say so. It took a great deal to shock Ivan the Terrible.

The Protestant world was not only shocked but frightened. In England, memories of the burnings in Mary Tudor's reign were still very much alive. A work called Foxe's *Book of Martyrs* helped to keep these memories vivid. Now, Englishmen started to ask themselves if the days of persecution might come back again.

The massacre also brought fears for Elizabeth's own safety. Two years earlier, just after the Northern Rebellion, the Scottish Protestant leader, the Earl of Moray, had been assassinated. Now the French Protestant leader was dead as well. Elizabeth was urged to take up a strong position to try to ensure her own safety. Once again, the cry rose up of "Cut off the Scottish Queen's head."

As so often before in moments of crisis, Elizabeth reacted extremely calmly. The French were beginning to feel that they had let their enthusiasm run away with them, and the French ambassador asked to be allowed to explain the massacre to her. She kept him waiting three days. When at last she received him, she was dressed in the deepest black. She was surrounded by grave-faced councillors, and supported by her full retinue of court ladies. Her manner was distant and chilly. When the ambassador stammered his explanations, she was dignified, but totally non-committal.

Soon it became clear that the Massacre of St Bartholomew would not be repeated elsewhere in Europe, at any rate for the time being. Elizabeth could feel justified for not having taken a stronger line against France. She had no wish to make France an enemy at a time when her relations with Spain were deteriorating. At the same time, she was having to deal with a great many Englishmen who were passionately anti-Catholic, and were not very interested in the wider aspects of foreign policy. In order to keep to her moderate, middle way, she needed a great deal of confidence in her own powers to govern.

This was just what Elizabeth had. Now, in her late thirties, she was no longer quite the same person who had come to the throne. Something of ardour and eagerness had been lost. At twenty-five she might have hoped to marry to please both herself and England. Now those days were past, and her office as Queen came first. She had gained in her cool, disillusioned ability to see things as they really were. The sheer power of survival, which she had always had, had been strengthened by all her troubles. Her life had become one of rigid self-discipline, combined with specific outlets of violent self-indulgence. One outlet was her rages. These were accepted, if feared, by the Court, because her father had raged in just the same way. The fact that her language, at such times, was vulgar and coarse did not worry her contemporaries. Her other great outlet was her flirtations. Time and again, she made a fool of herself with pretty young men. Yet after the early rumours about Leicester nobody had much doubt that it was Elizabeth who laid down precise limits as to when the fooling must stop.

While Elizabeth had been changing, England had changed as well. She had come to the throne of a small north European country that had lost its last continental possessions. She had given the country stability, and helped to unite it. With an increase of confidence at home. the English suddenly started to look overseas.

Traditionally, England had traded with neighbouring countries. While the ships of Spain and Portugal were sailing across the Atlantic, and, in the 1520s, right round the world, a typical English voyage was across the Channel or the North Sea. It was not until the 1550s that Willoughby and Chancellor were the first Englishmen to reach Moscow. Three years after Elizabeth came to the throne, a merchant called Anthony Jenkinson travelled through Russia to Persia. At the Persian court he was not allowed to wear his own shoes, because they were thought unfit to touch the ground, and the "Shaw" reproached him for being an unbeliever, that is a Christian. In spite of this, he managed to open up a new market for English cloth.

The important change came with voyages to the west. Spain and Portugal had already built up huge empires in Central and South America. They were growing rich from trade and from the fantastic gold treasures looted from ancient civilizations. A Papal Bull had divided the whole of the New World between them, and they were determined to cling to their monopoly. The French had tried to upset this situation by raiding in the West Indies, but the English had done very little apart from fishing in Newfoundland. Until Elizabeth's reign, the one English merchant to have traded across the Atlantic was William Hawkins the elder of Plymouth, father of William and John.

Then, with Elizabeth's reign, the English showed that they did not intend to accept this Spanish and Portuguese stranglehold on the Americas. Cecil told the Spanish ambassador, "The Pope hath no right to partition the world and give and take kingdoms to whomever he pleased." Elizabeth, with her ever-keen interest in finance, was prepared to subsidize voyages in the hope of a profit. It might prove one way of keeping her Navy afloat. Besides that, she was aware that there was a growing intellectual interest in exploration. Having a lively mind herself, she was ready to listen.

Much of the early interest in exploring came from a strange man called Dr Dee. In some ways Dee was a mediaeval figure. He was, in effect, Elizabeth's court magician. He advised her on astrology, man's future as shown by the stars. It is impossible to say whether Elizabeth believed in this, since no one has ever discovered what she really believed about anything. He also advised her on alchemy, the art of trying to turn base metals into gold. This may have appealed to Elizabeth, who was never one to neglect any chance to make money. In spite of all this, Dee was forward-looking in many ways. He was a distinguished mathematician and geographer. Through his friendship with the famous Mercator, he was up-to-date with the most recent geographical ideas of the day.

So politically, commercially, and intellectually, the English were ready to challenge Spain in America. All that they needed was a man. He appeared: thirty years of age, son and brother of prosperous merchants, and speaking with the broad accent of Devonshire. His name was John Hawkins of Plymouth.

Like so many great Elizabethans, from the Queen herself downwards, Hawkins was a strange mixture of qualities. He had a strong streak of the pirate and much of his trade was in African slaves. He was a scrupulous, highly responsible public servant. From 1562 onwards, he began to trade between the West Africa and the Spanish colonies in the Caribbean. His first expedition was in the nature of "flying a kite", to see whether Spain would allow English traders. The Spanish confiscated two cargoes of hide and sugar to try to discourage him.

Elizabeth intervened, but could not succeed in getting the cargoes released.

Hawkins next sailed in 1564. Elizabeth contributed a large and imposing ship called *Jesus of Lubeck* and allowed him to fly the royal standard. When Spanish officials questioned him in the West Indies, Hawkins was able to say he had sailed "by order of Elizabeth Queen of England whose fleet this is". The voyage was a great success, and pleased Elizabeth by making a profit of sixty per cent on the outlay.

When Hawkins set out again in 1567, she lent him two ships from the Navy, *Jesus* and *Minion*. He sailed from his home port of Plymouth, which was rapidly acquiring a new importance. Being right in the far west of England, it was an ideal starting-point for the Atlantic. All too soon, Hawkins became aware that, whatever other qualities the Queen might possess, she knew nothing at all about ships. *Jesus* was the pride of the Navy, a broad-beamed vessel with an enormous superstructure to make her look like a floating castle. In an inland sea, like the Baltic or Mediterranean, she might be adequate. Out in the mid-Atlantic, she climbed to the crest of the waves with as little grace as a cow climbing out of a ditch, then crashed down into the trough with a sickening lurch. Being so wide, she was hard to steer; being so top-heavy, she kept on nearly capsizing.

Once in the Caribbean, the voyage went from bad to worse. Hawkins had to use force to get the Spaniards to trade with him. Then he put into the harbour of San Juan de Ulua in Central America in order to repair *Jesus*. The authorities promised him a safe conduct. They then set upon the English, and sank all but two of their fleet. *Jesus* was captured. Hawkins fled into *Minion* and struggled back across the Atlantic with hardly any food. The voyage was agonizing, and more than four-fifths of the men on board died. Young Francis Drake, in his tiny ship, *Judith*, managed to reach home as well. Both men were alight with hatred for Spain, and so were the common seamen of Devonshire. In the close-knit society of the West country, the events of San Juan de Ulua were a personal blow. Elizabeth had unleashed a much greater force than she knew when she let the men of this remote and often neglected part of her kingdom challenge the mightiest empire in all the world.

The gloves were now off. The English were ready to fight for England and for Protestantism. Hawkins sailed off to help the French Protestants in La Rochelle. Later the same year, the gentry of Devon sent troops to help them, including young Walter Ralegh, aged seventeen.

Late in 1570, Elizabeth allowed Drake to sail once again for the Caribbean. In theory, Drake was working for Hawkins, and Hawkins worked for the Queen. In practice, as everyone would discover, Drake worked mainly for Drake. His first expedition was merely to spy out the land. Then in 1572, he set sail from Plymouth once more. His intention was nothing less than to seize the Spanish treasure which they brought every year from their colonies in Peru. At once, he entered into that world of high romance which it was his particular genius to inhabit. He climbed a tall tree and became the first Englishman ever to gaze upon the Pacific. He made an ambush by night. Once, when he needed to fetch help, he sailed for miles through mountainous seas on a make-shift raft with biscuit sacks for a sail. On his voyage home, his ship was so full of treasure that he used gold for a ballast. The people of Plymouth rushed out of St Andrew's Church in the middle of morning service to welcome him home.

Elizabeth was somewhat less delighted. She was hoping for better relations with Spain, and she thought it advisable for Drake to disappear quietly for a couple of years. She had no doubts at all about the financial advantages of the expedition. She had done very well indeed from the money that she had invested. Elizabeth's financial shrewdness was becoming famous in Europe. Although England was a small country, foreign bankers would lend her money at half the rate of interest that they charged to Philip of Spain who had all the wealth of the Americas to support him.

Soon, she had other projects in view. Martin Frobisher sailed with her blessing in search of the North-West Passage. This was a sea-route round North America to the Pacific which Dee and the other geographers were convinced must exist. His lack of success did not stop them from putting forward another theory. Mercator suggested there must be a vast continent in the South Pacific to balance the weight of the countries up in the north. Richard Grenville, another Westcountryman, wanted to go and find it. If Elizabeth let him it would mean that, for the first time in history, English ships would be sailing in the Pacific.

Long and tedious negotiations were started. As so often before, Elizabeth was divided. Her political sense told her that it would be dangerous to challenge Spain in the Pacific. Her financial sense was aware of the advantages to be gained. Then there was that other side of her nature, so often suppressed, that lit up at excitement and daring. Elizabeth never quite allowed it to sway her, but she could be stirred by the exploits of her great seamen.

In the end, she licensed an English captain to sail into the Pacific. She named not Grenville but Drake. He was already backed by a powerful syndicate which included Leicester and two men of fast-growing importance, Walsingham and Christopher Hatton. John Hawkins, soon to be Treasurer of the Navy, played a prominent part. Then Elizabeth herself joined the backers. Later, it was believed that she saw Drake in private to talk over his plans. Drake implied this was so. Elizabeth would only remark, "The gentleman careth not if I disavow him." As ever, she kept her own counsel as to what there might be to disavow.

In fact there was nothing. Drake's voyage was a triumph that increased the whole stature of England. He made his way through the bleak and winding passage at the tip of South America that is called the Straits of Magellan. Then gales tossed him southwards so that he shouted out he was further south than any man in the history of the world. He sailed up the coast of South America, seizing treasure from Spanish ships on the way. He swept on up the North American coast, and went further north than anybody had ever been in the Pacific. On his way home, he paused to claim California for the queen.

Then came the point when he disobeyed his orders. Everyone had expected him to sail back through the Straits of Magellan. Instead, he launched out across the Pacific. For sixty-eight days, he was out of sight of land, "as a pelican alone in the wilderness". No one had ever sailed so far, except for Magellan, and he had then been killed by Pacific natives. Drake survived. When he sailed into Plymouth Sound in November 1580, he was the first captain in history to have sailed his ship round the world.

Suddenly, doubt struck him. He had been away without any news for three years, less twelve days. England might now be in the power of his own mortal enemies. His first question to some fishermen was, "Is the Queen alive and well?"

The Queen was alive and well, and she knighted Drake. With this one voyage, the whole horizons of English life had suddenly become wider. Yet Elizabeth could not but realize that England was still an insignificant country compared to Spain. Only a few months before, Spain had annexed Portugal and all her overseas territories. Philip was now the most powerful man upon earth since the days of the Roman Empire.

There was one possible answer to this, which was for the English themselves to found colonies overseas. The impulse for this came once again from a group of Westcountrymen, all closely linked by their common interests and a succession of inter-marriages. The first was Sir Humphrey Gilbert. In 1578, Elizabeth gave him a patent to occupy any lands in America not already possessed by a Christian prince. In other words, she was not risking trouble with Spain. She was also a little doubtful about Gilbert himself, and called him a man of "no good hap by sea", that is unlucky. Unfortunately, she proved right. After many delays in starting, Gilbert finally reached North America. He took possession of Newfoundland, which thus became England's first colony overseas. He was drowned on his journey home.

Gilbert's work was carried on by his half-brother, Walter Ralegh, a charming and handsome young man who had recently come to court. Gossips were quick to comment that the Queen still had a very keen eye for handsome young men. "Two years ago he could scarcely keep one servant, and now with her bounty he can keep five hundred." Not all the Queen's bounty went into lavish living. Ralegh spent a great deal of it on schemes for colonization.

His great interest was in that part of America north of the Spanish territories but still far enough south to have a warm pleasant climate. He sent a prospecting expedition to what is now North Carolina. It brought back glowing reports and inspired a poem by Michael Drayton.

> When as the luscious smell
> Of that delicious land
> Above the sea that flows
> The clear wind throws,
> Your hearts to swell
> Approaching the dear strand.

Ralegh wanted something more concrete than poetry: heavy investment by Elizabeth. He persuaded his friend Richard Hakluyt to write a pamphlet on colonies meant for her eyes alone. No one was better qualified. Hakluyt was both a scholar and an enthusiast. He helped to inspire English voyages, and he left behind him a wonderful collection of vivid first-hand accounts of discovery and exploration. If anyone could have convinced Elizabeth, it would have been Hakluyt.

He did not succeed. The whole scheme was very new, and Elizabeth always wanted a guaranteed return for her money. Colonies in America would lead to trouble with Spain. She refused to share Hakluyt's conviction, which came out on page after page, that war with Spain was inevitable. The most she would do was to let the new territory be called Virginia, in honour of her unmarried state. Meanwhile, she continued to favour Ralegh. It could even be it was typical of her to like to do things indirectly.

In 1585, Ralegh sent out a second expedition, commanded by his kinsman, Sir Richard Grenville. It left behind a group of a hundred and seven men who stayed in America for a year. In 1587, another party of colonists, this time including women and children, went to Virginia. They became known as the "lost colony", because their fate is a mystery. Elizabeth must have congratulated herself on not laying out money or staking her own prestige on a lost cause.

Looking back, it now seems that Elizabeth lacked vision. It was Ralegh who said of America, "I shall yet live to see it an English nation." To have such a faith in those early days required singleness of purpose. Such a quality was valuable in a subject. It might have been dangerous in a queen.

CHAPTER ELEVEN

CARES OF STATE

"Princes, like suns, be evermore in sight,
All see the clouds betwixt them and their light."
Michael Drayton, *England's Heroical Epistles*.

Her palaces were thronged with people. There were officials and councillors. At times there were representatives of that somewhat troublesome body, the House of Commons. There were the men that she liked, a long succession of gifted and sweetly-spoken young men, with Leicester, now middle-aged and by no means as slim as he had been, a more or less permanent fixture. There were her court ladies, with whom she discussed theology as well as the latest fashions. Through them all swept Elizabeth, high heels clacking, heavy dress swishing, the material stiff against her thin, pale skin, the skirts belling out from her narrow waist. As she grew older, she became even more imperious. When she so much as lifted her long, nervously sensitive fingers, everyone had to come running.

Her moods were like sun and storm. She could rage and cajole by turns, could give sharp orders and then retreat into an agony of indecision that made her advisers despair.

Among all the crowds, she was essentially solitary. Her ministers were, in the last resort, advisers only. Like the modern President of the United States, and unlike the modern Queen of England, she had to be head of government as well as being formal head of state.

The young men were diversions. There were limits as to how far she had trusted Leicester, and nobody since had come to take Leicester's place. The ladies were there to provide society, not to be close companions. Few other people in the world were so cut off from intimate human contact; so condemned to carry a burden from which only death could release them. By an irony, one of the few was Philip of Spain, who chose to live monk-like and solitary in his palace of the Escorial. Another one was the Pope.

It would have been so easy to look for a way out: to do just what people advised her rather than stop and argue: to dedicate herself to a popular cause and be borne along by a great wave of mass emotion. Instead, amidst all her shifts and hesitations, she clung to her own ideas. In a world which resorted to violence as a quick solution, she always sought peace. While one extreme produced another extreme, and opposite factions were pushed ever further apart, she looked for a middle way. At times it must have seemed an impossible task: the slender figure of one lonely woman trying to hold back all the gale of the world.

At home, a new word was being heard, "Puritan". The Puritans were men who wished to reform the Church of England and make it more radically Protestant. They rejected all compromise as being what John Knox, that master of picturesque phrase, had called a "mingle-mangle". All features which linked the Anglican Church to historic Christian tradition were to be scrapped. The Prayer Book, with its ancient prayers, was condemned as being "culled and picked out of that Popish dunghill, the Mass book, full of abominations". Special vestments for clergy "and such like baggage . . . are as the garments of the idol". Services were to be replaced in part by "Prophesyings". These were ardent revivalist meetings in which groups of people met to confess their own bad conduct and to accuse others.

All this was very foreign to the traditional English way of life, often frowned on by earnest foreigners as being frivolous and easy-going. One of Shakespeare's roistering characters said on being told that somebody was a Puritan, "O, if I thought that, I'ld beat him like a dog!" Elizabeth was much more interested in the political implications. The Puritans claimed the right of all church members to choose their own ministers. In an age which believed that authority was passed on in successive stages from those at the top to those set underneath them, this meant quite literally turning society upside down. She looked on the extreme Puritans much as a modern government looks upon extreme revolutionary students.

She was ready to come to terms with more moderate forms of Puritanism. This was proved by her choice of Sir Francis Walsingham to join Burghley as her second Principal Secretary in 1573. Walsingham had strong Puritan sympathies without approving of violence or disorder. Like Burghley, he was both able and dedicated. Her gift for selecting advisers was one of Elizabeth's greatest assets as a queen. She also had the gift of inspiring service and loyalty. Infuriating as she could be at times, they served her gladly, and in the last analysis, loved her.

One aspect of Elizabeth guaranteed to irritate any man was her attitude to marriage. At long last her advisers started to resign themselves to her perpetual spinsterhood. This being so, Elizabeth let it be known that she might get married after all.

The trouble with Elizabeth was that nobody knew her well enough to be certain what she was thinking. She baffled those closest to her as much as she baffles people today. What made it so hard to tell if she was serious was the nature of her new choice. The young gentleman was more than twenty years younger than she was. Nor was he typical of Elizabeth's follies, for he was badly disfigured by smallpox. He was the youngest son of the French royal family, known as the Duke of Alençon.

Alençon first came to Elizabeth's notice when he was sixteen. At that stage, he was merely a substitute for his nineteen-year-old brother whom she rejected as being too firmly Catholic. She had not met him. Startled English observers in Paris were reduced to counting the pock-holes on the end of his nose, and wondering how long it would take him to grow a real beard.

The scheme lasted long enough for Elizabeth to conclude a defensive treaty with France. She hoped that this would balance the threat from Spain. Then in 1572 came the Massacre of St Bartholomew, which put paid to any idea of a French marriage. The scheme was revived in 1579, not by Elizabeth but by Alençon himself.

Like all her other suitors, he started to woo from a distance. He bombarded her with passionate letters, and sent his closest friend, Simier, to do his wooing. Elizabeth enjoyed this enormously. All her particular favourites had their nicknames. Leicester had long been her "Eyes", and Christopher Hatton her "Lids". Walter Ralegh was "Water", or anything to do with water. In no time at all, Simier became "Monkey". For a little, her courtiers watched indulgently. Flirtation was a hobby with Elizabeth, as needlework might be with some other women. Then, an alarming suspicion began to strike them. What if she were in earnest?

It was at this stage that Alençon showed an enterprise that none of her other suitors had ever displayed. He disguised himself and sneaked over to England. Elizabeth was enchanted.

He was a comic little man, and Elizabeth promptly nicknamed him her "Frog". So far as anyone could make out, which, with Elizabeth, was never very far, she genuinely enjoyed his society. Alençon was an adventurer by nature. It began to look as if Elizabeth's notorious weakness for high-spirited men would prove even stronger than her equally notorious weakness for handsome ones. When he went home after thirteen dizzy days in Elizabeth's company, everyone was beginning to wonder. Was she really going to get married at last?

The situation started to split the country. Among her Councillors, Burghley, with great firmness of purpose, clung to the view that he had held for so long. Elizabeth ought to get married to secure the succession. She was, however, already forty-five. Those who opposed the marriage, such as Leicester and Walsingham, could point out that she might not now have children. Even if she did, it might, at the then stage of medical knowledge, endanger her life. They could also, with their own Protestant sympathies, point to the strong feelings against her having a Catholic husband.

Feeling came to a head when a Puritan called John Stubbs published a pamphlet called *Discovery of a Gaping Gulf wherein England is like to be swallowed by another French marriage*. The language was violent, indeed outrageous, and Elizabeth flew into a fury. Normally it was her close associates who had to suffer her temper. This time, she lashed out wildly at one of her subjects. Under an act passed to protect Philip II of Spain on his marriage to Mary, she condemned Stubbs and his publisher to have their right hands cut off in public. Stubbs behaved very bravely, crying out, "God save the Queen" when the act was done. There was no doubt whatsoever from the way that the crowd reacted that this was one of those rare times when Elizabeth was completely out of touch with public opinion.

She realized this. Ever since she had come to the throne she had been determined that her marriage would never divide the country. She raged and she wept: but she did not marry Alençon. It is possible that the tears were quite genuine. Until now, she had always kept her options open.

This time, she was finally saying goodbye to the idea of marriage and children, and with it a final goodbye to her own youth. Then came another blow. Simier disliked Leicester as an arch-opponent of the Alençon marriage. It was he who out of sheer malice revealed to Elizabeth what a number of people knew but nobody had dared tell her. Leicester himself had got married in secret the year before.

1579 was a bad year for Elizabeth as a human being. 1580 showed ominous signs that it would be a bad year for her as a queen. Since Philip had annexed Portugal, Spain was more powerful than ever. Worse still for Elizabeth, who cared so deeply for unity in the country, was the new menace from within.

Ever since the Pope had released her Catholic subjects from having to obey her, Elizabeth had faced a situation in which all Catholics were potential traitors. For the Catholics themselves, it was a tragic position. They were still Englishmen, like any others. They had the normal attachment to some particular place; to a huddle of roofs, or a busy street, to ploughed fields, or a clump of trees on a hill. They had friends and neighbours who shared their lives. Many of them loved Elizabeth. They had turned out to greet her if ever she passed near their homes, they had shared the general pride in a Queen who kept England at peace. Now they were suddenly wrenched apart from normal English life. At best, they could hope to live quietly and withdrawn. At the worst, they faced ugly deaths.

The first Roman Catholic priest to be killed in England was Cuthbert Mayne who, in 1571, was hounded to death by that extreme Protestant, Richard Grenville. A few years later, the situation became more urgent. In 1580, Philip II outlawed the Dutch Protestant leader, William of Orange, and put a price on his head. In the same year, the Cardinal Secretary wrote to Madrid giving a ruling on whether it would be sinful to murder Elizabeth. "There is no doubt that whosoever sends her out of the world with the pious intention of doing God service, not only does not sin but gains merit, especially having regard to the sentence (*of excommunication*) pronounced against her by Pius V of holy memory." To make the situation even more clear it was specifically stated that this dispensation to murder Elizabeth applied not only to foreigners but to her own Catholic subjects.

Against this background, the Catholic Church sent the Jesuit mission to England. The Jesuits were all hand-picked men of great intellectual gifts, who had undergone many years of rigorous spiritual training. They had been made to imagine, in detail, the prospect of torture and martyrdom. At least one of them, Edmund Campion, was a man whose abilities could have won him high office in England if it had not been for his devotion to his religion.

The English authorities chose to look on the Jesuits as a political threat. What mattered to them was that the Catholics had threatened to kill Elizabeth, and that her sudden death could endanger the safety of the whole nation. To make things worse from their point of view, the leader of the mission, Robert Parsons, was a man who was essentially a politician and propagandist.

So Campion and Parsons became hunted men. They went to the country houses of known supporters, and there, in darkness and secrecy, they said Mass for the household. Sometimes a few more people crept in from the farms and villages nearby. There was always the risk that a neighbour would denounce them. From time to time, the Jesuits had to take quick refuge in "priest-holes", tiny cubby holes hidden behind wall panels or in the angle of stairs. It was from such a priest-hole that Campion was betrayed by a narrow chink of light where the panel had not been pulled back completely. He was taken to London where he refused to recant his views, although he knew that a very ugly death waited for him. To the end, he affirmed that his sole motive had been religious, and that politics had no part in his mission. "We travelled only for souls," he cried on the scaffold. There is no reason to doubt him, for Campion had a greatness of spirit that is one of the more attractive features of an age when religion seemed so often to bring out the worst in people.

The English indeed had good reason to fear. Already both Moray, the Scots Protestant leader, and the French Protestant leader had been murdered. Then in March 1582, the Dutch leader, William of Orange, was shot through the face and severely wounded. Small wonder that the English trembled for Elizabeth's life. They wished that Elizabeth would be more fearful herself. "Nothing in the world grieveth me more," Leicester lamented, "than to see her majesty believes that this increase of Papists in her realm can be no danger to her." Above all, the existence of Mary acted as a bait to those who wanted to see Elizabeth dead.

So long as she was in England, so long would plots be woven about her. Mary herself may not have started them, but, bored with the tedium of her life, always impulsive rather than reasoning, optimistic in improbable circumstances, she was willing to join in. "The poor fool will never cease until she lose her head," her brother-in-law Charles IX of France had exclaimed on hearing of one of her schemes. Some of her other French relations were willing to give her active support, so, of course, were Philip of Spain and the Pope. It was now no longer a question of her right to the succession but of her immediate claim to the throne itself.

It was a world of spying and counter-spying. Walsingham, who was in charge of English intelligence, had the traditional qualities of a blood-hound. His agents stopped a man travelling as a dentist, who turned out to be a messenger of the Spanish ambassador. He was carrying letters hidden in the back of a looking-glass. They revealed a scheme to get rid of Elizabeth, the so-called "Enterprise of England". In order to find out more about this, Walsingham managed to intercept secret letters between Mary and the French ambassador. In fact, he was on the wrong track, and learnt little more about the Enterprise. He did read Mary's suggestions of how she could continue to correspond if she knew she was being watched. She suggested that the ambassador write in alum which would only become visible when it was heated, or that he send her messages inside the high heels of shoes.

Then at the end of 1583, Walsingham's agents found more positive evidence. It led them to Francis Throgmorton, a young Catholic member of a well-known family. He had been corresponding with Mary and had supplied the Spanish ambassador with a list of places where foreign forces could land, as well as of Catholics likely to help an invasion. The ambassador was expelled, not to be replaced. He left breathing revenge and traditional Spanish pride. "I pray that God ... will give me grace to be his instrument of vengeance, even though I have to walk bare-footed to the other side of the world to beg for it." Throgmorton died in the Tower.

Elizabeth could not delude herself that the trouble was over. In the winter of the Throgmorton Plot, a young Catholic gentleman from Warwickshire set out to kill her, and to see "her head set upon a pole, for she was a serpent and a viper". He, too, ended in the Tower. Elizabeth could ignore him as a crackpot, but she could not ignore the increasing danger of Mary. She, so slow to condemn Mary, was moved at last to say, "All this shows that her intention was to lull us into security that we might less seek to discover practices (*treasons*) at home and abroad."

She was still not ready to throw Mary to the Protestant
wolves. After the Throgmorton Plot she placed her under
closer confinement. She still used her powers of censor-
ship to forbid violent propaganda against Mary. When
Burleigh wrote *The Example of Justice in England*, which
defended strong measures against Catholics on political
grounds, Mary was not mentioned. This is a strong
contrast to the Catholic literature which vilified Elizabeth
and exalted Mary to the position of a near-saint. Sometimes the Catholic propaganda justified the killing of
Elizabeth, as did the *Defence of the English Catholics* by
William, later Cardinal, Allen.

Another plot against Elizabeth, involving a Member of
Parliament, failed. It seemed all too likely the next
plot would succeed. In July 1584, William of Orange,
champion of the Netherlands against Spain, was shot dead
in Delft. His vision of a united Low Countries, in which
Protestant and Catholic could live in freedom together,
was never to be fulfilled. As a rich young man leading a
pleasant, indeed lavish, life, he had come to oppose the
religious tyranny of Spain in the Netherlands. "However
strongly I am myself a Catholic," he said, "I cannot
approve of princes attempting to rule the consciences of
their subjects." Events forced him to identify himself with
the Protestant cause, but he had an essential belief in the
freedom of human conscience that was ahead of his time.
He was one of those men by whose death mankind is the
poorer.

Among Elizabeth's subjects, his death strengthened
fears that she, too, might be murdered. The Privy Council
formed the Bond of Association to try to defend her.
It said, in effect, that if Elizabeth were killed the signa-
tories would take action against anybody who benefited
by her death. In practical terms this meant that they
would destroy Mary Queen of Scots, whether or not she
had any part in Elizabeth's murder. Many thousands of

people signed it. Elizabeth must have had some idea what was going on, but kept aloof from a violent scheme so foreign to her whole nature.

William's death raised another problem: what would become of the Netherlands? He had no obvious successor. It is possible that the Dutch might have invited Elizabeth's opportunist suitor, Alençon, to become their ruler, but he had died of fever a few weeks before. Elizabeth had been genuinely upset by his death. "Melancholy doth so possess us as both public and private causes are at a stay for a season," commented Walsingham.

She was in no mood to accept when the people of the Netherlands invited her to become their sovereign in William's place. She had too much to do at home. In any case, she never wished, at any stage, to expand her kingdom. "My mind was never to invade my neighbours, or to usurp over any; I am contented to reign over mine own, and to rule as a just prince." On the other hand, she had no wish to see Spain overrun the Netherlands, only to use it as a jumping-off point for invasion of England. As a compromise, she offered to send forces. These were to be led by none other than Leicester.

The Dutch received him joyfully.

> Blest be that Virgin Queen that sent this good,
> And blest be he that comes to save our blood.

It did not take long for the affair to turn sour on Elizabeth. Her courtiers were treated to a classic display of temper when news came that "that she-wolf", otherwise Leicester's wife, was going out to the Netherlands too. Even more important, Elizabeth was a woman who likes to see a clear return for her money. Leicester was unable to achieve anything decisive, and she came to feel as if she was just tipping good English gold into the endless watery dykes that intersect the Low Countries. Soon she was "weary of the charges of war". Besides, it might be imprudent to antagonize Spain too far. As always, Elizabeth wanted peace.

The campaign in the Netherlands petered out. It is now chiefly remembered for the death of Leicester's nephew, Sir Philip Sidney, from a wound which he received at Zutphen. The situation returned to a troubled, uncertain peace: strained relations with Spain, and the uneasy presence of Mary.

CHAPTER TWELVE

"STRIKE OR BE STRUCK"

"The daughter of debate, that eke discord doth sow,
Shall reap no gain where former rule hath still taught
peace to grow.
No foreign banished wight shall anchor in this port;
Our realm it brooks no stranger's force, let them
elsewhere resort."

Queen Elizabeth I (of Mary Queen of Scots).

Was there any answer to the problem of Mary? Was there anywhere she could be sent where she would not be a constant threat? There was one possible ray of light. Mary had now been so long in England that her son, James, was practically grown up. Could he provide a way out of the dilemma?

James was a precocious and learned youth, aptly described as being "an old young man". In later years, the contrast between his display of learning and a basic lack of political judgement would become all too apparent. For the moment, he was an unknown quantity.

To Mary herself, he was her only child, never seen since babyhood, whom she still loved and yearned for. These feelings were so natural to her that she assumed he must share them. To Elizabeth, he was a possible means of escape from one of her greatest problems. If she let Mary free, could James act as a guarantee for her good conduct? It could be made clear to him that what was at stake was his own right of succession to the English throne.

So Walsingham was sent to negotiate with James. Their talks improved relations between England and Scotland, though the wheels of negotiation had to be greased with what Walsingham called "oil of gold". As ever, he had a difficult time to persuade Elizabeth to pay up. The talks helped to lull any new English fears of invasion by their back door. They did nothing at all about Mary.

What neither Mary nor Elizabeth had allowed for was James himself. He had no affection at all for his mother, whom he did not remember. His Protestant tutors had done their work well: he looked on her primarily as the woman who had plotted the death of his father and then married the murderer. What he did have was a very strong sense of his own importance and the value of his position. There was no doubt at all where his priorities lay. "How fond and inconstant I were if I should prefer my mother to the title," he was later to write to Leicester. Elizabeth's hopes were dashed. A young man of this temperament would be the last person in the world to take a notorious trouble-maker off her hands.

James's rejection of his mother was a step nearer to tragedy. In the whole nature of the situation, one or other of the two women was doomed. Sooner or later, something would inevitably spark off disaster. The only point at issue was: which of the two would die?

The English were determined it should not be Elizabeth She was already protected by the Bond of Association. Now Parliament sought to give the Bond legal force by passing a Bill for the Queen's safety. Once again, Elizabeth came into conflict with both her Councillors and the Commons. Once again, their complaint was that she did not take a violent enough attitude.

The new Bill allowed that if there was any plot against Elizabeth, commissioners could investigate how far a claimant to the throne was involved. They would then have the right to pronounce sentence of death. Although she was not mentioned by name, it implied that Mary would be considered a party to plots on her behalf. She would never be allowed to succeed to the English throne. Then came another case of Elizabeth blocking extreme measures. She refused to allow the Bill to be extended to James, unless he was proved to have a direct part in her assassination. This ensured that James, more and more emerging as the one likely heir to the throne, could succeed without difficulty. It also ensured that the Scots would have no interest in joining in plots against her. The Commons passed these amendments with the utmost reluctance. Anything that lessened the force of the Bill seemed to be a gamble on Elizabeth's safety.

The Act for the Queen's Safety became law in March 1585. Next time there was a plot against Elizabeth's life, the English had some legal sanction for dealing with Mary. It was not very long before the occasion arose.

Mary, so out of real touch with the world outside, had never ceased to hope for some escape from her sad situation. She was not kept in close confinement, but, as a woman who loved society and physical exercise, her life was exceedingly irksome. After having been all through her youth at the centre of great events, she felt cut off from the world. It is not surprising that she snatched at any chance of writing to her friends. After over a year, during which she had had no outside letters, she discovered a new chance for secret correspondence. At that point, she was confined in a house that, unlike many great houses of the day, had no brewery of its own. Beer for the household was delivered there once a week. By bribing the brewer, Mary arranged to have letters sent to her inside the kegs of beer. The letters would be put in small waterproof containers that could be inserted through the bung-holes. Her own letters would go out with the empty kegs. What Mary did not know was that one of the men she trusted had already betrayed her to Walsingham, and that Walsingham was paying the brewer as well.

In this way, Mary received a large back-log of letters which had been kept for her by the French ambassador. They gave details of the "Enterprise", the scheme to kill Elizabeth. Mary, naturally enough, was delighted at being in touch with friends. She wrote back, getting her secretary to use a cipher. Walsingham already had the full details of it.

All Walsingham had to do was to wait, convinced that sooner or later Mary would deliver herself into his hands. The means came through a young Catholic gentleman called Anthony Babington.

Babington wrote to Mary about schemes to rescue her. To achieve this, England would be invaded by Catholic armies and the English Catholics would rise in rebellion. In order to succeed, it would be necessary to get rid of Elizabeth. Mary's reply was eager. All she asked for was that her rescue should be so timed as not to endanger her. After so many years of imprisonment, her first thought was for freedom. It is impossible to tell just what she really thought about killing Elizabeth. Certainly, it would have been typical of Mary to act impulsively on events as they affected her personally, rather than to look at their full political implications.

Walsingham was not worried by the question of whether or not Mary had any personal malice towards Elizabeth. With this letter, she had condemned herself. His attempt, by means of a forged postscript, to discover the names of other plotters had failed, but that was a minor issue. He now had specific grounds for accusing Mary of plotting against Elizabeth. This meant, under the recent Act, that her life could be forfeit.

From this point, events moved inexorably forwards. Both women were now caught up in a situation from which they were powerless to escape. Elizabeth, who seemed to have everything to gain, was as much the victim of circumstance as Mary, the destined loser. While both her nobility and the common people of England rejoiced that Mary, "the bosom serpent", was at last delivered into their hands, Elizabeth was plunged into a spiritual abyss.

In October 1586, Mary was taken to Fotheringay Castle in Northamptonshire. There, in the great hall, she was put on trial before thirty-six commissioners who included Walsingham, Burghley, and Sir Christopher Hatton. She was allowed nobody to defend her. The tense and heightened atmosphere of the time, in which no one could be impartial, meant that her judges were her accusers as well. Naturally, Mary denied the charges of plotting against Elizabeth's life. She knew her own life was at stake.

Mary was now a fat, round-shouldered, middle-aged woman, with cropped grey hair hidden underneath her red wig. Time, and the strain of captivity, had robbed her cruelly of her beauty. Yet somehow, for the first time since she had left France, she regained a true dignity. This was no longer the woman who had "howled" at John Knox, who had made such a disastrous mess of her life with Darnley and Bothwell, who had fretted and pined for so long in captivity. For the first time, the "beautiful and more than beautiful" girl whom Ronsard had praised was growing to her full stature.

Elizabeth was diminished. Almost alone she, on whose own brow the coronation oil had been spilt, was aware of the enormity of what was being done. Ten years later, one of Shakespeare's kings was to cry out on the stage:

> Not all the waters in the rude, rough sea
> Can wash the balm from an anointed king.

Elizabeth's lawyers declared that what they were doing was legal under Act of Parliament. In any case Mary, having signed her own act of abdication, was no longer a queen. Elizabeth might agree intellectually, but something, as if in her very blood and her bones, protested.

Mary was found guilty. Then started a passionate campaign in Parliament to have her executed. Christopher Hatton who, like Leicester, was an old favourite of Elizabeth's, matured into a politician, spoke vehemently against her. She was "the hope of all idolatry" whose way of life had been "most filthy and detestable". "Her ambitious mind, grounded in Papistry" had "thirsted after this crown". His words and feelings were echoed by many more.

Elizabeth agonized. She, normally so active, lay late in bed and was reluctant to see Burghley. A deputation from Parliament managed to see her, and begged her not to have too many scruples about executing Mary. "She is only a cousin to you in a remote degree. But we be sons and children of this land, whereof you be not only the natural mother but also the wedded spouse. And therefore much more is due from you to us all than to her alone."

Elizabeth promised that she would soon give them an answer. She told them how unhappy she was, being "so clear from malice . . . that one, not different in sex, of like estate and my near kin, should be fallen into so great a crime." There is no reason to doubt her distress. A genuine sense of mercy was one of Elizabeth's most attractive qualities as a human being. Now it was being combined with that indecisiveness and reluctance to take firm action that was her greatest liability as a queen. Her predicament was described by Spenser:

> But she, whose Princely breast was touched near
> With piteous ruth of her so wretched plight,
> Though plain she saw by all, that she did hear,
> That she of death was guilty found by right,
> Yet would not let just vengeance on her light.

Some form of action was needed. The situation could no longer be solved by Elizabeth's doing nothing. In December, she consented to a public proclamation of the death sentence against Mary. Walsingham kept on trying to force the issue and get her to sign the death warrant. It was not until February 1st 1587, that she finally did so. It was nearly four months after the trial, and Walsingham himself was then ill in bed. "The grief thereof," said Elizabeth with grim humour, "will go near to kill him outright."

At last, she had been driven into taking a definite action, because the alternative was even more unthinkable. "Suffer or strike, strike or be struck," she muttered. Even then, she was looking for a way out. Could Mary be dispatched from the world by some easier means than judicial execution? She made Walsingham sound Mary's gaoler. "God forbid that I should make so foul a shipwreck of my conscience," he replied piously. As he had been one of the party who had howled for Mary's death in the first place, Elizabeth was not pleased. By one of the many ironies of the time, it was Elizabeth's opponents, such as the King of France, who favoured putting Mary to death in secret, if she had to die.

As soon as the warrant was signed, Burghley sent it off. There was no delay. On February 7th, Mary was told that she must prepare for death the following morning.

Next day, she was led into the great hall at Fotheringay, where a scaffold had been made ready, draped with black. Upon her, had descended that strange sense of liberation that often comes at the end of a long period of tension. There was nothing else left for Mary except to die bravely and unprotestingly in the Catholic faith. That, she told the Dean of Peterborough, who fussed round her urging her to change her religion, she was going to do.

She took off her outer clothes, and laid her head quietly on the block. Her last words, repeated several times, were,

"Into thy hands, O Lord, I commend my spirit." Then the axe fell. The second blow severed her neck. Her red wig fell off, and one of her little dogs which had been hidden under her skirts, huddled against her shoulders as if for comfort. In the end, it had to be dragged away.

In her death, Mary Stuart rose to a level that, in life, she had never known. Men who were boys when she died would be old men when the same tragic pattern was repeated in the life and death of her grandson, Charles.

Elizabeth could not face the consequences of what she had done. She stormed that she had not meant to kill Mary. With a blind impulse to shift the burden of guilt, she blamed those who had taken the message. Mary's death was an admission of failure. For nearly twenty years, she, by her own will-power had kept Mary from execution. At last, she had surrendered, but the reality of what had happened was too harsh for her to bear.

Maybe she herself had walked to the scaffold, and died with Mary in her imagination. It was an age when remembrances of death, the skull under the painted face, were brought continually to people's notice. It was an age of sudden diseases for which there was little cure. A poem written a few years later, called *In Time of Pestilence*, expressed the ideas of death and decay which haunted Elizabeth's subjects. At times, they must have haunted Elizabeth too.

> Beauty is but a flower
> Which wrinkles will devour;
> Brightness falls from the air;
> Queens have died young and fair;
> Dust hath closed Helen's eye;
> I am sick, I must die—
> *Lord, have mercy on us!*

CHAPTER THIRTEEN

WAR

"You follow Drake by sea, the scourge of Spain,
The dreadful dragon, terror to your foes,
Victorious in his return from Inde,
In all his high attempts unvanquishèd.

. . . . .

You fight for Christ, and England's peerless queen
Elizabeth, the wonder of the world,
Over whose throne the enemies of God
Have thundered erst their vain successless braves.
O, ten times treble happy men that fight
Under the cross of Christ and England's queen."

George Peele, *A Farewell to the Generals
of our English Forces, 1589.*

Elizabeth had retreated into a state of nervous paralysis, afflicted by even more than her usual indecision. Meanwhile, a new situation was coming about. With the death of Mary, who had had Tudor blood in her veins, English Catholics had to face the fact that any new Catholic claimant to the throne would be very clearly a foreigner. They would have, more than ever before, to choose between their church and their country.

The man who emerged as a new claimant was Philip II of Spain. His claim, which was supported by the exiled Catholic leader, William Allen, was based on the fact that he, like Elizabeth, was descended from Edward III. The Spanish ambassador in Paris declared that it was "God's

obvious design" for Philip to unite the crowns of England
and Spain. This pleased Philip who, as he grew older,
was becoming increasingly religious. Elizabeth, who
remembered him as her sister Mary's young and reluctant
bridegroom, might not have recognized the monk-like
figure who spent hour after hour on his knees in prayer
and meditation. What came from his prayers was a belief
that God wanted him to invade England.

The fact that Philip was their new champion solved
the dilemma of most English Catholics. Good churchmen
they might be, and their number contained men and
women prepared to die for their faith, but few except
those who had already gone into exile wanted to see
England ruled by Philip. What, a few years before, had
threatened to be a religious conflict dividing the nation,
was turned into a national one that united it.

There were two views as to what should be done about
this new Spanish menace. Heading one was Elizabeth.
She kept obstinately to her policy of seeking peace. Her
temperament, in this as in religion, led her to look for
moderation and reason. Because of her sex, she had never
been brought up in the common masculine idea that there
is anything glorious in battle and bloodshed. Her complete rejection of the notion that warfare is glamorous
belongs more to our age than her own. Her experience in
what she called the "sieve" of the Netherlands war had
shown her how one can pour out money to very little
avail. She had no wish at all to become involved in some
wider enterprise which might undo nearly thirty years'
work of her endless, pettifogging exertions to keep her
country solvent.

She was supported by Burghley, who was always ready
to put out peace feelers. Opposed to them were those who
thought war was inevitable. There was Walsingham, that
ardent Protestant, to whom politics were a form of
crusade. He was always demanding money for some

enterprise he saw as essential. Time and again, to his fury, Elizabeth refused. There was Drake, eager, at times uncontrollable, with his unmatched gift for inspiring the loyalty of the common seamen. There was the Treasurer of the Navy, John Hawkins of Plymouth, who was using both his merchant's acuteness and his hard-won knowledge of sea-faring to improve the state of the English fleet. These men were cast in a bolder, in some ways a more generous, mould than Elizabeth, and they were irked by her caution and peace-seeking. Yet it was she who had placed and who kept them in positions of trust. She could have chosen nonentities who would have obeyed her automatically. Instead, she seemed almost to be compensating for the limitations of her own nature. She would go to almost any lengths to avert a crisis, but, if it became inevitable, she had men who could rise to meet it.

While Elizabeth was busy trying to keep the peace, above all trying to stop any danger of France and Spain combining against her, she was ready to give her hotheads a certain amount of licence. In Francis Drake, the son of a poor tenant-farmer turned Protestant lay-preacher, she had a man who was willing, indeed eager, to challenge, single-handed, the mightiest power on earth. Nor was this mere foolhardiness on Drake's part. His sea-faring exploits had made his name dreaded on both sides of the Atlantic.

So Drake set off for Spain to harry the great invasion fleet, or Armada, which was being made ready to sail against England. Elizabeth gave him permission to go so far as "distressing their ships within their havens". Then she suddenly changed her mind, and sent orders to stop him. Drake was already nine days out of Plymouth. He, who according to fast-growing legend, could track down any ship in the world, was impossible to catch at sea. Could it be that Elizabeth, even at the moment when Burghley was assuring the Spanish authorities that Drake was acting without her permission, knew perfectly well that this was just what would happen?

This was the start of an expedition that proved amazingly daring, even for Drake. He sailed into Cadiz harbour in Spain and held it for thirty-six hours against the Spanish fleet. He left, having sunk or burnt nearly forty ships. The psychological damage he did was even greater. He then, with frightening bravado, sailed up and down the Spanish coast, raiding and burning the barrels in which the stores for the Armada were to have been carried. Before he sailed home to Plymouth, he captured a huge Portuguese ship, three times the size of his own largest vessel, with a cargo worth over £100,000. This was a fortune. He left behind him a still stronger legend of Drake the invincible.

The war party now sought for one final, killing stroke, Elizabeth was still hoping for peace. She refused to keep her Navy permanently at full fighting strength, and saved thereby £2,433 18s 4d every month. In terms of what it could buy at that time, this was a very respectable sum. Elizabeth knew far better than Drake what was needed to balance the country's budget, even down to the fourpence. Besides, she knew that an outright war with Spain could have a disastrous effect on the country's traditional wool trade. Some of those who now shouted loudest for war with Spain might be the first to regret it. She compromised by such cheaper preparations as having a chain of beacons set up to give warning if the Spanish fleet approached.

As so often with Elizabeth's parsimony, there was more sense to it than her exasperated servants were prepared to admit. Providing food for men on shipboard was a major problem. Many an expedition had eaten up most of its supplies while still kept in harbour by gales. Once at sea, lack of fresh food, especially of fresh fruit and vegetables, quickly caused a loathsome disease called scurvy. Had she kept her Navy at sea for months on end, in a defensive role, the men's health would soon have been wrecked. Nor was she letting them waste their supplies of powder and shot before they were needed. It was worth-while letting some of her sea-dogs fret.

One man whom she had allowed to go his own way was John Hawkins, Treasurer of the Navy, who for ten years past had been building up England's fighting fleet. In the process, he had made enemies: those who had been en-riching themselves in the past at the country's expense, and those who doubted his new and controversial ideas. The fact that he had stayed in office for so long, amid fierce attacks, was another case of Elizabeth's supporting a good public servant.

What Hawkins did was to change the whole design of English ships. His own unhappy experiences in *Jesus of Lubeck* had made him realize that ships needed to be narrower and more stream-lined, with less of the heavy superstructures that made them roll in rough seas. In ten years, he had built a navy to his own specifications. His ships were more quick and manoeuvrable than any warships yet seen, and he mounted them with guns on both sides. This was a complete change from the idea, handed down since classical times, that warships were floating castles made to carry soldiers. The traditional way of fighting at sea was to board the enemy ships and engage in hand-to-hand combat. Hawkins was making a revolu-tion in naval warfare.

At last, in the spring of 1588, Elizabeth allowed her fleet to get ready. Ships from London and the Medway ports tacked down the Channel against the prevailing south-westerly winds. They anchored in a small, insignificant-looking port built of cold, grey stone, with a name that was fast being taken all over the world.

Upon the British coast what ship yet ever came
That not of Plymouth hears, where the brave navies lie?

In Plymouth, they were a very long way from London. It was over two hundred miles to the west, further than Elizabeth had ever been in her life. The quickest way of carrying news was for a man to ride a succession of horses, changing whenever one tired. The roads might be deep in mud, for all through the late spring and early summer it rained, with that relentless English rain that seeps through a man's clothes and into his bones. Down in Plymouth, the seamen fretted and grumbled. They explored the dark, cobbled alleyways round the harbour, and swore when they slipped on fish-heads or rotting food. Their leaders talked and drank with the Mayor, William Hawkins, elder brother of John. At seventy, he had worked day and night through the winter to see that all the ships based in Plymouth were scraped clean of the weed and barnacles which grew on their wooden sides. All the time, seamen and leaders had one thought uppermost in their mind. When would Elizabeth, in faraway London, act?

So far, she had done very little. She had commanded that look-outs should "ply up and down" in some place where they could cover all the approaches to England, Scotland, and Ireland. That gave scope for some wry amusement at the expense of a woman who imagined there was such a place. She had appointed Lord Howard of Effingham, the Lord Admiral, to command her fleet in action. This had caused some surprise, not least to the Spaniards to whom the words "Drake" and "the English Navy" meant exactly the same thing. As with so many of her decisions, there was some wisdom behind it. Howard had great prestige, and everyone would obey him. Drake was so much of an individualist that some other captains would have resented his orders. Besides, there was always the faint, nagging risk that Drake might use the entire English Navy for purposes of his own.

At long last, Elizabeth decreed that they might go

out and seek the Spaniards. Howard, Drake and John Hawkins wasted no time. For weeks past, the south-westerly winds had kept them cooped up in Plymouth Sound for days on end. They seized the chance of a north-easterly, and sailed down towards the Spanish coast in hopes of intercepting the Armada before it reached England. Then the wind turned against them. It would be hard for them to reach Spain, and, in the meantime, the Spanish fleet could be blown towards England. They turned back for Plymouth.

When news finally came that the Spanish fleet had been sighted off the Isles of Scilly, it took the English by surprise. They found themselves caught in Plymouth Sound by the tide which pours fiercely into the mouths of the Plym and Tamar. The wind was blustering in from the sea as well, so they could not manage to take their fleet out until they had the force of the outgoing tide to help them. This may well be the hard fact behind the legend of Drake's refusal to leave until he had finished his game of bowls. That night, the beacons blazed forth on the heights above the Sound. The watchers who saw the glow lit more beacons, and so the news was carried eastwards and westwards to the boundaries of Elizabeth's realm. The Spaniards were coming.

The English fleet began to slip out of the Sound when the tide had turned. Lowering clouds obscured the night sky. Next morning, a gale was blowing, and squalls of rain sometimes cut visibility down to a few yards. The watchers on the shore found it hard to make out what was happening. Now the whole future of England was in the hands of her seamen. It was those in London who were now fretting for news.

News was slow to come. The English had gained an early advantage by slipping round to the rear of the Spanish fleet, so that they were first to catch the westerly wind in their sails. To everybody's surprise, the Spanish ships had sailed on without trying to put into Plymouth. In fact, they were aiming to sail right up the Channel to rendezvous with Spanish troops in the Netherlands before invading England.

Reports came in that the Armada was slowly sailing up-Channel, drawing inexorably nearer and nearer to London. Nothing seemed to have happened, except that Drake was rumoured to have captured a Spanish ship and everything aboard her. Then off Portland Bill, and again off the Isle of Wight, there were short encounters. Though not even Hawkins and Drake may have fully realized it, this was the beginning of a new era of naval warfare: battle by guns, not soldiers. It was so new to both sides, that neither could aim at all accurately and both started to run short of ammunition. The English had the advantage of nimbler ships, but even so the engagements had to be called inconclusive. The Spanish fleet anchored off Calais.

Every day brought them closer to their troops in the Netherlands. The English had to do something to stop their slow and majestic progress. As night came down, Howard sent eight tall ships to drift with the tide on to the Spanish fleet. The ships were loaded with cannons with their muzzles packed tightly with shot. Once they were moving, the English sailors scrambled hastily off the ships. The last men on board set the rigging on fire. As they reached the Spanish fleet, they were blazing all over. The heat made the guns explode, and shot scattered in every direction.

The fire ships began the end of the Spanish Armada. It was to live on, a broken but still gallant fleet, to sail round the far north of Scotland and to be battered by terrible storms. Some of the ships were flung on to the west coast of Ireland and wrecked.

While the fleets were at sea, the English had been getting ready by land. Leicester was mustering forces, having, as he put it, to "cook, cater and hunt" for his entire army. Eleven days after the Spanish fleet had first been scattered at Calais, Elizabeth sailed down to Tilbury to inspect her forces.

So far, she could feel she had been successful. The Armada was still in the North Sea, but it had not invaded England. It had been kept off with less outlay of men and money than everyone had assured her was possible. Above all, there had been no rising of her Catholic subjects. Burghley had warned her of "secret treasons of the mind and heart". Walsingham, that alarmist, had wanted extreme measures against suspected Catholic supporters. Elizabeth had been sceptical. She was not herself a person in whom religion was an overmastering motive, and instinct had told her that such people were an exception among the English. She proved right. As a rather minor poet was to say of the Spanish Armada:

> Even Catholics (that erred name doth please the
> Papists) were
> As foremost in the quarrel as the foremost arms
> to bear.

When Elizabeth reached Tilbury, she rode out to review her forces. She progressed slowly through every part of the camp. Her guard, in this era when so many Protestant leaders had been assassinated, was two little boys, one carrying her helmet and another leading her horse; three horsemen; and one man on foot. She was dressed in white velvet, with a breastplate more for decoration than for protection, and was bare-headed. On one side of her rode a bulky, white-haired figure, her once-handsome love, Leicester. On the other side, was a graceful young man, Leicester's step-son, the Earl of Essex.

Elizabeth was transformed. It still happened to her sometimes, as it had when she was a girl. She dithered, and she hesitated, she refused to act, she acted and then she changed her mind, she drove everyone to distraction;

and then suddenly she was changed. She stopped being an ageing woman wearing a wig and a dress much too young for her, and she became instead, blazing and incandescent, the very symbol of England. It was like a chemical change that could be brought about in her by moments of strong emotion, and by the love of her people flowing out almost visibly to her.

In such a mood, Elizabeth delivered her most famous speech.

"I know that I have the body of a weak and feeble woman, but I have the heart and stomach of a king, and of a king of England too, and think foul scorn that Parma or Spain, or any prince of Europe should dare to invade the borders of my realm; to which, rather than any dishonour should grow by me, I myself will take up arms, I myself will be your general, judge and rewarder of every one of your virtues in the field."

Her forces listened to her. They were a typical amateur English army: landowners, ploughmen, shopkeepers, tailors and downright villains. They were muddled, bewildered and grumbling. Had they been called on to fight, they might, like other English armies before and since, have amazed themselves even more than their enemies by their courage and spirit.

They had not wanted to be in the army. In war, glory went to the leaders. Politicians, who stayed safely home in London, might blame Elizabeth for not having sought war in the past. No ordinary Englishmen would. To the common soldier, war meant at the best the risk of losing an arm or a leg. It might mean a sword through his guts. Yet now that, against her will and theirs, they were involved in fighting, Elizabeth was raising them all to a level above themselves. In that moment, the Queen was themselves, they were the Queen, and all together were England.

CHAPTER FOURTEEN

GLORIANA

"The rose is red,
The leaves are green,
God save Elizabeth
Our noble Queen."

Anon.

Few women have ever attracted such a torrent of praise. Some of it was realistic, and came at times from improbable sources. "She is certainly a great Queen," said Pope Sixtus V, "and were she only a Catholic she would be our dearly beloved. Just look how well she governs! She is only a woman, only mistress of half an island, and yet she makes herself feared by Spain, by France, by the Empire, by all."

Much of the praise has the air of being more artificial. It may be concerned with Elizabeth's importance as a ruler, when Sir John Davies wrote:

To that clear Majesty which in the north
    Doth, like another sun, in glory rise;
Which standeth fixed, yet spreads her heavenly worth,
    Lodestone to hearts, and lodestar to all eyes.

Other writers, such as Sir Philip Sidney, had stressed her intellectual and moral powers:

Her inward worth all outward show transcends,
Envy her merits with regret commends;
Like sparkling gems her virtues draw the sight,
And in her conduct she is always bright.

Ralegh spoke of the idea that she did not age:

In heaven queen she is among the spheres,
She mistress-like makes all things to be pure;
Eternity in her oft change she bears;
   She beauty is, by her the fair endure.

Time wears her not, she doth his chariot guide.

Spenser wrote of her beauty:

See where she sits upon the grassy green,
   (O seemly sight)
Yclad in scarlet like a maiden Queen,
   And ermines white.
Upon her head a crimson coronet,
With damask roses and daffodillies set:
   Bay-leaves between,
   And primroses green
Embellish the sweet violet.

Tell me, have you seen her angelic face,
   Like Phoebe fair?
Her heavenly haviour, her princely grace,
   Can you well compare?

There was a poetic cult of Elizabeth, the virgin-goddess.
Her classically-minded poets gave her names like Cynthia
and Phoebe that are associated with the moon-goddess, or
called her Diana, implying a virgin huntress. Some people
have thought that the cult of Elizabeth gained its strength
because, since the Reformation, English people missed the
worship of the Virgin Mary. In fact, worship of a female
figure is very much older than Christianity, and the moon-

goddess, with whom Elizabeth was identified, goes back to the very origins of religion.

What lies underneath this cult? Is there any real connection between the poets' Cynthia, "Such as all womankind did far excell" and a middle-aged woman called Elizabeth Tudor? At first sight, it all appears rather absurd, especially since most of the poetry was written in the second half of Elizabeth's life. She did not age gracefully, and the heavy, harsh cosmetics of the day did little to help. Nor did the lack of good dentistry. All through her life she liked to gobble up sweet things. Perhaps she craved the instant energy that they gave her. She paid for it with black teeth. For much of her life she wore a wig which was patently artificial. Age, which had made her father gross, exaggerated her thinness. Her sharp nose and chin began to grow nearer to one another, until she looked like a witch. To modern readers, the idea of calling her a goddess appears not only absurd but a little pathetic.

Modern readers have not met Elizabeth and portraits can only convey her outer appearance. There seems to be no doubt at all that, when people actually met her, she made an enormous impact, and that what she actually looked like was somewhat irrelevant. Her father had made a similar impact, her predecessor and her successor did not, so it was not simply a question of holding high office. It means that she must have possessed that kind of magnetism, which is an almost physical gift, which some people, such as some actors and some politicians, undeniably have. As is common with such people, Elizabeth had great vitality which made her able to carry on when others were tired, and she retained her qualities into old age. To this extent the poems are simply stating a fact: Elizabeth was a woman completely out of the ordinary.

At times, she impressed people by her sheer intellectual powers, which were so much above those of the normal monarch. She was able to sway even such hardened bodies as deputations from the House of Commons. Her courtiers cherished the memory of how, when the Polish ambassador had been impertinent to her, she had thoroughly trounced him in extempore Latin.

She also impressed those to whom intellect meant very little. All through her reign she loved to go upon progresses, and in her late sixties she bade "the old stay behind, and the young and able go with her". At such times, she enchanted the common people of England. Her position was almost like that of a celibate priest who rejects close family ties for a wider love. This was the one personal relationship of Elizabeth's life which was supremely successful: her relationship with her subjects. As Sir Christopher Hatton said, "The Queen did fish for men's souls and had so sweet a bait that none could escape her network," or, in the words of the Mayor of Coventry, she had "the hearts of all your loving subjects".

The impact upon the country of such a woman was enormous and yet hard to calculate. We cannot say exactly what part Elizabeth had personally in inspiring the astonishing achievements of her reign. For Elizabethan England was one of those great ages when life is lived on a larger scale than in common times.

Certainly, Elizabeth helped to create the conditions. She brought peace and stability at home and abroad. She brought peace of mind to her subjects by what was, for the time, an unusual lack of religious persecution. She kept a tight grip on the country's finances. Her miserliness and fussiness over expenditure are not appealing qualities in themselves, but her subjects did not object to them, whatever her minsters said. In the last resort, it was her subjects' money that she was saving.

Combined with this, she ruled over a brilliant court, to which most of the gifted men of the day were attracted. It provided a place for exchanging ideas, and was the sort of surroundings in which the imagination suddenly

catches fire. The cult of Elizabeth, virgin-goddess, artificial
in many ways as it was, provided a focus for achievement.
She was in herself the symbol that England was free,
united, and prosperous.

There are two ways in which Elizabethan England far
excelled previous ages. The first is in the exploits of her
seamen, recorded for ever in Hakluyt's splendid collection.
In terms of actual achievement, they have been equalled,
indeed surpassed, but no group of men ever did more to
stir the imagination. They lived magnificently, as did
Drake in the moment when he lauched himself across the
unknown vastness of the Pacific. They died magnificently,
as did Gilbert when he cried out in his tiny ship in the
wild Atlantic, "We are as near to heaven by sea as by
land," or Grenville, when he fought on in the *Revenge*
so that, "the Spaniards should never so glory to have
taken one ship of her Majesty". They knew the joys of
discovery, as when Amadas and Barlow, Devon men like
so many others, first landed in the New World. "We
found the people most gentle, loving and faithful, void of
all guile and treason, and such as live after the manner
of the golden age."

Elizabeth was a financial power behind many of these
voyages. She used the results of them as a weapon in her
diplomacy. For ten years, she supported John Hawkins in
building his new model navy. Towards the end of her
reign she granted a charter to what was to be the most
influential trading company ever formed: the East India
Company.

The other way in which the Elizabethans excelled all
previous ages was in the writing of poetry. There had
been English poets before, most notably Chaucer, but
suddenly, in the second half of Elizabeth's reign, there
came a moment like that in the early summer when all
the birds start to sing together at dawn. Everybody wrote
poetry: courtiers and men of action like Sir Philip Sidney

and Ralegh, civil servants like Spenser, the Queen herself. It was not a minority activity, indulged in by young men who could not fit in with society, but a part of life.

The fact that literature was fashionable amid the brilliant life at court also helped the drama. Elizabeth delighted in plays, and they became a part of most great festivities. When Elizabeth visited Leicester at Kenilworth in 1575 she was entertained for nineteen days by plays and pageants as well as by fireworks, hunting, music, and Latin orations. In the previous year, she had granted Leicester a patent to let his servants act plays. With such patronage in high places, the theatre began to attract brilliant young men in a way that it never had before. There were wits from the universities, such as Christopher Marlowe, and likely young men from the provinces. One of them made enough money to purchase a coat of arms and to retire to his small native town as the principal citizen. The plays that he wrote in the process are the very peak of Elizabethan achievement. He did not write in isolation. It needed the Elizabethan age to produce a Shakespeare.

The very air of the time must have stimulated a young man of genius. The English language itself was something fresh and fascinating, as so many other poets were showing. New things were always happening, whether new forms of architecture in great country houses like Longleat, or new sounds being written by men like Tallis and Byrd. Intellectually, too, it was an age of discovery. It was an Englishman, Thomas Harriot, who expanded the whole horizon of mathematics. All these forms of activity reacted on one another, for poets, musicians, scholars and architects did not live in their separate little worlds. They were still close enough for that great scientific enquirer, Francis Bacon, to say, "I have taken all knowledge to be my province."

Shakespeare reflected the liveliness of the age, and its

exuberance. Many of his characters are on an immense, heroic scale.

> His legs bestrid the ocean: his reared arm
> Crested the world.
>   I that with my sword
> Quartered the world, and o'er great Neptune's back
> With ships made cities.

We cannot call her winds and waters sighs and tears, they are greater storms and tempests than almanacs can report.

> Age cannot wither her, nor custom stale
> Her infinite variety.

To the Elizabethans, such characters were not exaggerations. Was the Queen herself, was Drake, to be measured in mortal terms?

He also showed the Elizabethan love of visual beauty, especially in small details like flowers and precious stones which are shown so beautifully by the miniature painters of the day, Hilliard and Oliver.

> O, she doth teach the torches to burn bright,
> Her beauty hangs upon the cheek of night
> Like a rich jewel in an Ethiop's ear
>
>   Look how the floor of heaven
> Is thick inlaid with patines of bright gold.
>
>   Violets dim
> But sweeter than the lids of Juno's eyes
> Or Cytherea's breath.

Shakespeare wrote of love for an England that had triumphed over its foes:

> This precious stone set in the silver sea,
> Which serves it in the office of a wall,

Or as a moat defensive to a house . . .
England, bound in with the triumphant sea.

At the same time, he knew the men of England's reluctant armies:

Can honour set-to a leg? No. Or an arm? No. Or take away the grief of a wound? No. Honour hath no skill in surgery then? No.

And this same half-faced fellow, Shadow,—give me this man: he presents no mark to the enemy,—the foeman may with as great aim level at the edge of a penknife. And, for a retreat,—how swiftly will this Feeble, the woman's tailor, run off!

Shakespeare wrote of terrible English weather, like that in Armada year, when nobody could tell if it was summer or winter:

The green corn
Hath rotted ere his youth attained a beard,
The fold stands empty in the drownèd field.

At times he may have referred directly to things that had happened. Hamlet attacking his mother may mirror the feelings of James towards Mary Queen of Scots:

A bloody deed?—almost as bad, good mother,
As kill a king, and marry with his brother.
Such an act . . .
Makes marriage vows
As false as dicer's oaths.

He referred to exploration, and the strange wonders seen by travellers:

The cannibals that each other eat,

and to a magical isle

full of noises
Sounds and sweet airs that give delight and hurt not.

The isle was Bermuda, where a shipload of travellers outward bound for America had been wrecked.

In one play, nominally set in ancient Greece, Shakespeare gave the classic statement of the Elizabethan belief in order:

> The heavens themselves, the planets, and this centre,
> Observe degree, priority, and place,
> Insisture, course, proportion, season, form,
> Office, and custom, all in line of order . . .
> Take but degree away, untune that string,
> And hark, what discord follows!

He showed the traditional fear, which so haunted Elizabeth herself, of what would happen if order collapsed, and everyone could cry out:

> Chaos is come again.

There was one theme on which Shakespeare never revealed his feelings, that was religion. We do not know what Elizabeth thought of religion, in her innermost heart, so it is appropriate that her greatest subject should keep his silence as well.

CHAPTER FIFTEEN

THE LAST ATTACHMENT

"A man of a nature not to be ruled . . . I demand
whether there can be a more dangerous image than
this represented to any monarch living, much more
to a lady."

Francis Bacon of Essex.

Suddenly, she was growing old. Of course, she refused
to admit it. Her physical vigour was very little abated,
and she still danced as "high and disposedly" as in the
days when she had been so determined to prove that the
Queen of Scots was not the only fascinating woman in
Europe. Her dresses became, if possible, more ornate and
fantastic than ever. Once the French ambassador, in a
state of some disbelief, reported that her neckline was so
low that one could see right down to her navel. But Time,
of which Elizabethan poets were all so conscious, had a
cruel way of reminding her that it was passing. Her
friends and contemporaries were starting to die.

Leicester had died of a fever just after the Armada. She
kept a letter he sent her and wrote HIS LAST LETTER
on it. Her sorrow was great. If she could have loved anybody completely, it would have been him. Then in 1590,
Walsingham died. "There is good news here," wrote the
King of Spain, but to Elizabeth it was the loss of a faithful
servant. In 1591, she lost another with Christopher
Hatton, who had danced his way into her favour and
lived to become a successful Lord Chancellor. Burghley

remained, but Burghley was growing old. In another decade or so he would be shown on the London stage as that sententious old bore, Polonius. The young men might laugh at him, but Elizabeth, who had worked with him from the beginning, was aware of his incomparable worth.

Who was there to take their place among the young men to whom, though she might not admit as much, she appeared as an old woman? There was Walter Ralegh, poetic and dashing, with that strong physical magnetism that meant so much to Elizabeth. But Ralegh was not of the stuff of which statesmen are made, and in the long run this probably counted for more against him than the fact that, to Elizabeth's predictable fury, he had made one of her Maids of Honour pregnant. Then there were two men, ten years or so younger than Ralegh. They could not have been a greater physical contrast. There was Robert Cecil, Burghley's younger son, undersized and hunch-backed. Elizabeth called him her Pygmy. There was the Earl of Essex, Leicester's step-son. He was handsome, graceful, and daring: the very pattern of the men who had always been able to stir Elizabeth.

Behind Cecil was his father. Burghley's eldest son had proved a great disappointment, and all his hopes now rested on this puny young man. Behind Essex were Burghley's two nephews, Francis and Anthony Bacon. Francis had one of the keenest intellects of the age and, at a time of great writers, wrote some of the finest prose. He was disappointed that Burghley had not singled him out, so he fixed his hopes to the rising star of Essex. Essex, he knew, was inordinately ambitious. On the face of it, he was bound to win over Cecil.

Peace at home was going to be disturbed by the jockeying for position between these two young men. Elizabeth was not fated to live at peace with her neighbours either. After the Armada, tension with Spain continued. Philip was said to have vowed that "he would spend his candle to the socket, but he would be revenged and have his will of her (*Elizabeth*)". To make himself better able to fight he was rebuilding his fleet with lower, narrower ships "after the mould and manner of the English navy". John Hawkins could have asked for no greater tribute.

In 1589, Elizabeth reluctantly gave leave for an expedition in which Drake and Essex took part. Its aim was to destroy the part of the Spanish fleet based on Portugal, and to restore the Portuguese Pretender, Don Antonio, to his throne. It ended in chaos. Little damage was done to the Spanish fleet and the Portuguese showed no signs of wanting Don Antonio back. The English captured a great many barrels of wine. It soon became very obvious, by the sailors' behaviour, that they had captured far too many barrels of wine. Then, as so often happened on voyages in those days, the men became sick. By the time they got home to Plymouth, up to eight thousand, more than half of the original number, were dead.

In 1591, ships were sent to blockade the Azores to stop the Spanish fleet bringing treasure home from America. Sir Richard Grenville, another of that group of West-countrymen who had brought so much glory to Elizabeth's reign, was vice-admiral of the expedition. At a time when no other English ship was ready or willing to fight, Grenville alone, in the *Revenge*, took on the entire Spanish fleet. Inevitably, he died of his wounds in the end. It was action as brave as Thermopylae, and as magnificently insane as the Charge of the Light Brigade. Sir Walter Ralegh told the story in marvellous prose.

A greater loss was to come. In 1595, Drake and Hawkins sailed together from Plymouth on an expedition intended to capture the Isthmus of Panama from the Spaniards. Within five months of sailing they had both died at sea: the man who had built the English fleet and the man who, more than anyone else, had given English sailors their fighting spirit. It would be two hundred years before seamen would find in Nelson a hero to match with Drake. As for the ship that sailed into their home port with the news that Drake and Hawkins were dead, it was surely the saddest vessel ever to come past Rame Head into Plymouth Sound.

Not even the loss of such men could stop the struggle with Spain. As a proof of Philip's enmity, Essex had uncovered a plot by a Portuguese Jew called Lopez who was Elizabeth's own doctor. According to Essex, Lopez had been bribed by Philip to poison Elizabeth. The evidence was uncertain, and Elizabeth, loyal as so often before to her servants, did not want to believe it. Even when Lopez had been found guilty by a commission, she refused to sign his death warrant. In the end, so far as can be told, it seems that Essex took him out of the Tower by a trick and had him executed.

Then in 1596, Essex rose to glorious heights. With Lord Howard and Walter Ralegh he went on an expedition to Cadiz. They burnt shipping and sacked the town. It was an act of splendid bravado, that seemed at the time more important than the Armada. "Great is the Queen of England!" cried people in Venice on hearing the news. "O! what a woman, if she were but a Christian!"

When Essex returned, he was the Queen's darling, another, maybe the last, in that line of handsome and daring young men who had made her reign glorious. He had found the way to her heart. She, poor, doting elderly woman who tried to behave like a beautiful girl of twenty, would do anything for this young and god-like man. So people whispered. But would she? Already she had disappointed Essex by not giving high legal office to Francis Bacon. While Essex was in Cadiz she had at last appointed a new Principal Secretary who would come to take Burghley's place. It was Robert Cecil, "Robert the devil", as Essex called him, the hunch-back. He had already been doing the work for five years. Elizabeth had not really changed very much. She had always delighted in letting men think they had got the better of her, but she always knew the exact moment when the play-acting had to stop.

Essex and Ralegh went on one more expedition together against Spain. The aim once again was to intercept the Spanish treasure fleet in the Azores. It ended in a muddle and achieved almost nothing. While they were away, and England was unprotected, reports came from Plymouth that a new Spanish Armada was nearing the Cornish coast. It was scattered by storms, but the whole episode left a sour taste behind.

This is reflected in the writings of a young lawyer and poet called John Donne, whom Essex took with him to Cadiz and the Azores. He wrote of the storm which scattered them early in their voyage to the Azores:

> Then note they the ship's sicknesses, the mast
> Shak'd with this ague, and the hold and waste
> With a salt dropsy clog'd, and all our tacklings
> Snapping, like too-high-stretched treble strings.
> And from our tottered sails rags drop down so,
> As from one hanged in chains, a year ago.

Poetry of this sort is a world apart from the madrigals sung to the praises of Gloriana. It was a sign of changes to come.

All around Elizabeth the world was changing. There was a new king in France, the Protestant Henry of Navarre, but such was the chaos in France that he did not even hold his own capital, Paris. He needed money, and Elizabeth, to avoid his overthrow by the Catholics, gave it to him. She was having to pay heavily in foreign aid, what with the Netherlands war and the money that young James VI of Scotland demanded to keep his good-will. Essex, in one of his death or glory moods, went off to help Henry in what proved to be an expensive and utterly fruitless expedition. It was painful to see the resources which Elizabeth had built up with such care and prudence so squandered. The irony was that Henry then turned Catholic in order to unite France. "Paris is worth a Mass," he was alleged to have said.

Elizabeth was to have no peaceful old age. Her money problems, and she was always one to be obsessed by money, were made worse by serious failures of the harvest in three years running. Thousands of her subjects were quite literally starving, and they roamed the countryside dressed in rags, terrifying more prosperous citizens. Farmers and tradesmen set their dogs on the beggars, but the haunting spectre of them remained. It was hard now to think of England as prosperous and secure.

The religious problem also remained to worry and nag at her. As well as her constant duel with the foreign Catholic powers there was Puritanism at home. Within a few months of the rejoicing over the Spanish Armada, an underground press had started to issue Puritan tracts. They were a lively and biting attack against bishops, signed by a man who called himself Martin Marprelate. Elizabeth saw them as dangerous. If bishops should be deposed, then the nobility might be; if the nobility, then herself.

As had happened before, one extreme of feeling produced another. The deaths of Leicester and Walsingham removed two men who had sympathized with the Puritans while remaining essentially moderate. These men had both had Elizabeth's confidence, and nobody took their place. The Archbishop of Canterbury, Whitgift, whom Elizabeth called her "black husband" was a stern disciplinarian, determined to keep order within the Church. The 1590s became a period of increasing opposition to Puritanism. It was a dangerous tendency. Anti-

Catholic feeling had helped to unite the nation, by link-ing religion to patriotism. The increasing split between the Established Church and the Crown on the one hand, and the Puritans on the other, might come to divide England.

All the time, death was drawing nearer. In 1598, Burghley died. Towards the end, Elizabeth fed him "with her own princely hand, as a careful nurse". It was one of those moments when she showed the warmth of a genuine human affection. Once she had told him that she only wished to live as long as she had him with her, and there may have been a strong grain of truth beneath the courtly exaggeration. It was now forty years since she, as a young woman, had chosen him to be her chief minister. They worked for so long together that it is hard, at times, to say just what had been done by Eliza-beth, what by Burghley. What is certain is that neither of them alone, neither of them with another partner, could have done so much. Amid all their stresses and disagree-ments, they had achieved a balance of mind and of temperament that made them one of the outstanding partnerships in all history.

A few weeks later, there came another death: Philip II of Spain. Elizabeth had met him when she was still a young girl. He had been her brother-in-law, her suitor, her ally, and then her deadliest enemy. Whatever role he had played at any moment, he had been an integral and inescapable part of her life. His death left an empti-ness.

While the others died, Elizabeth clung fiercely on to life. She danced and quarrelled with Essex, then went through the sweetness of making it up, as if she had been a young girl. Truly, it seemed as if this handsome young man might do anything that he wished with the doting old woman. He might have, if he had been wise. But Essex would not stop to study what Francis Bacon had called, "That deep and inscrutable centre of the Court, which is her Majesty's mind."

Elizabeth was above all, as her father had been, a monarch who expected to be obeyed. This had been obvious even when she was a young woman, and Melville had prophesied that she would never marry because "You may not suffer a commander." It became even more true as she grew old. Burghley had warned his son that, while he must always be ready to try to change Elizabeth's mind, in the last resort their relationship would be that of mistress and servant.

Essex, secure in his own youthful arrogance, did not realize this. "Cannot princes err? . . . Is an earthly power or authority infinite?" he exclaimed, and time and again he flouted Elizabeth. At times, she seemed to accept it, which made him more arrogant still, at other times she flew into one of her famous rages, and once boxed him hard on the ears. He had the capacity to make her feel violently, and, at her age to feel anything, even fury, was so much better than the terrible peace of being dead. Society was so dominated by men that it was accepted as natural that they should make use of women for their entertainment. It never occurred to Essex that Elizabeth had a very long history of making use of men.

Suddenly, after one of their fiercest quarrels, she found that she had another use for him. In theory, Elizabeth ruled not only over England and Wales but over Ireland as well. In practice, the English exercised a vague and uncertain government over the area around Dublin. The Irish were completely different from the people in England: in their culture, in their language, and in having kept to their Roman Catholic faith. Visiting Englishmen made the complaints that Englishmen visiting foreign countries so often make, that the people were very dirty and lazy, and treated their animals badly. On a more serious level, men like Ralegh and Spenser had spent years of their lives in trying to sort out the Irish problem, without any success. The Irish would not accept foreign rule, and the English could not impose it. Throughout Elizabeth's reign, Ireland had been like a running sore on the English body politic, what Bacon called "that ulcer of Ireland" that "hath run on and raged more".

Yet Elizabeth dared not abandon Ireland, if only because Philip of Spain might step in. Even after Philip's death there was still a strong risk of intervention by Spain. At this point, the Irish staged their most successful rebellion yet, under the Earl of Tyrone. Someone was needed to quell it, yet nobody wished to go, for as the Venetian ambassador said, "Ireland may well be called the Englishman's grave." Then Essex stepped in. He saw himself, by one splendid military stroke, solving the Irish problem, and so winning such glory as no Elizabethan had won before.

He was appointed Lord Lieutenant of Ireland, and he persuaded Elizabeth to give him an army. It was the greatest force that she raised during her reign, and she could ill afford it. On her part, the move was a desperate gamble. Nobody had yet succeeded in Ireland, maybe Essex would do so, driven along by the force of his over-weening ambition. Besides, given all this ardour and energy, it was better that it should be used to the service of England than frittered away. Essex might well be tamed into being a useful statesman, as others had been before him.

Essex had no idea of the size of the problems that faced him. He was not a man who looked at things realistically. The Elizabethans were given to picturesque language, and often used what seem like wild exaggerations to modern ears. Underneath the exaggerations, there might be a core of hard fact. Drake had boasted; but Drake could have sailed any craft ever built, through the trickiest seas in the world. With Essex, the boasting and the achievement were blurred, until even he may not have been certain which one was which. The only way he could justify the arrogant tone he had used to Elizabeth was by achieving something remarkable.

When Essex arrived in Ireland, he went on a sort of military progress. Like other progresses of the time, it was ruinously expensive, and it accomplished almost nothing. Elizabeth, for once in her life, chafed for action. Essex's failure to get any results was making the Earl of Tyrone look more important than he really was. Why she demanded, should the Queen of England "who hath held down the greatest enemy she had" be made to appear so powerless in the face of "a base bush kern (*an Irish soldier or peasant*)?"

There were other grounds for her anger. Essex, against her express commands, had started to dub knights. He was obviously trying to create a following with personal loyalty to himself. He had made the Earl of Southampton his General of the Horse, and Southampton had committed that classic Elizabethan crime of having married one of the Maids of Honour without Elizabeth's consent. Worse, he was still failing to do anything. In September 1599, Elizabeth wrote a devastating letter demolishing his excuses. "If the sickness of the army be the reason, why was not the action undertaken when the army was in better state? if winter's approach, why were the summer months of July and August lost?"

Even while she was brooding over this letter, Essex at last acted, if action it might be called. He marched towards Tyrone's forces and the two armies skirmished together without any real attempt to fight. Then Tyrone invited Essex to secret parley. The two men met at a ford, and Tyrone had to wade his horse into the water in order to talk to Essex on the opposite bank. Nobody knows exactly what they said to each other, though Tyrone later gave an unlikely account to the Spanish ambassador, and three soldiers who claimed to have eavesdropped behind bushes told stories which duly reached Elizabeth's ears. It is possible that they discussed what would happen when the aging Queen was dead, and agreed that Tyrone should rule Ireland while Essex took power in England, with James as a puppet king. For the moment, they concluded a truce.

It was a monstrously small result for such an expenditure of money, men and prestige. The only chance of persuading Elizabeth to accept it was for Essex to go to her in person and rely on the power that he had over her, the delight she had in his presence. He sailed back to England and then rode fast to Nonsuch Palace, where Elizabeth was holding her court. He burst in on her, covered with mud: an eager, vital, young man; a startled old woman caught without even the usual pretence of her red wig. She seemed delighted to see him. If he could get away with this, he could surely get away with anything. They dined at midday, and Essex appeared triumphant.

In the afternoon, Elizabeth saw Cecil. She was not just the doting old woman whom Essex had thought her. She was the girl who, at sixteen, had talked herself out of trouble when Seymour had lost his life. She was the young woman who had done anything for Leicester: other than do what Leicester wanted. She was the triumphant survivor of a thousand court intrigues. She was Cynthia and Diana for whom the poets had sighed, and when she meant them to, sigh they did, as Ralegh had found to his cost. She was the woman whom, for the last fifty years, every man on first meeting her had consistently underestimated, simply because she was a woman. And she was the Queen of England.

All that Elizabeth needed was time: time to make sure that Essex had not brought a whole army with him and that she was not faced with the onset of revolution. This done, Essex was summoned to explain his conduct of

Irish affairs to the Privy Council. He could give no satisfactory answer as to why he had made a truce, and why
he had come back to England without permission. That
night, he was confined to his room in the palace. Two
days later, he was in custody.

It was nearly a year before he out again. At last, he
was set free, with threats and an eleven-hour-long scolding from the Privy Council. Perhaps Elizabeth still hoped
to tame her wild thoroughbred, and break him into
serving the State. One way of doing this was to cut off
his supplies. "An unruly horse must be abated of his
provender, that he may be the more easily and better
managed," she said. She took away the revenue he had
enjoyed from customs duty on wine. When he wrote
"very dutiful letters" she commented sharply that "when
she took it to be the abundance of the heart, she found it
to be but a preparative to a suit for the renewing of his
farm of sweet wines".

Her technique did not work. Essex would not be
mastered. If he could not dominate Elizabeth, he would
depose her. He started to make wild comments which
stripped the last mask of pretence from their relationship.
"Being now an old woman," he said, Elizabeth "was no
less crooked and distorted in mind than she was in body."
In February 1601, Essex was summoned to appear once
again in front of the Privy Council. He allowed the
messengers into his house, but would not let them go
free. Soon afterwards, he rode out at the head of two
hundred men, crying out that his life had been threatened. It was a desperate bid to raise all his admirers in
London. Shots were fired in the City streets. Before evening came, he had surrendered.

This time, he had no hope. It was not just Elizabeth
who was against him, but Cecil, and Walter Ralegh who
blamed Essex for all his own disappointments. Essex
in turn had called Ralegh "the fox".

During the brief-lived rebellion, Elizabeth had behaved with great coolness. Such crises always brought out that streak of heroism buried beneath her caution. Now followed the sort of ordeal which she always found very much worse, the state trial of Essex for treason. Inevitably, he was condemned to death. Elizabeth was given the warrant to sign. This was the moment to set all her Councillors wondering. She had been so reluctant to sign Norfolk's warrant, and she had never loved Norfolk as she had seemed to love this golden youth. She had risked the whole safety of her kingdom rather than sign Mary Stuart's life away. How long would it take her to condemn Essex to death? The answer was five short days. Those around her commented that she seemed moved and distressed, but then all through her life the needs of state had warred with her private feelings. In the end, it was always the needs of state that had won. This was the first time, however, that she had not tried to fight the knowledge that death was inevitable. Did that mean that she, at last, was facing the fact for herself?

CHAPTER SIXTEEN

THE END

Mortality, behold and fear!
What a change of flesh is here!
Think how many royal bones
Sleep within this heap of stones . . .
For here they lie had realms and lands,
That now want strength to stir their hands . . .
Here are sands, ignoble things,
Dropped from the ruined sides of Kings.

> Lines on the Royal Tombs in Westminster
> Abbey, attributed to Francis Beaumont, but
> possibly by William Basse.

It was over forty years since she had come to the throne.
There were men and women now grandparents who had
known no other ruler. Not even the oldest man alive
could remember so long a reign. The previous one to sur-
pass it had ended over two hundred years before. In fact,
since the far-off days of the Saxons, only two kings had
ruled for longer than she had.

Inevitably, people were starting to look to the future.
After the drama with Essex, she herself took no further
part in the struggle for power, but let it take place around
her. Ralegh "that in pride exceeds all men alive" was
trying to fill the vacuum left by Essex. In vain, for Cecil
was clinging tightly to his position. His power was
greater than his father's had been, though his qualities
were less, for he did not have to share his power with

Walsingham, Leicester, and Hatton. More, he was determined to stay where he was, and that meant not merely that he must be accepted by Elizabeth, but by whoever came after her.

All these long years, Elizabeth had gambled upon her own survival. It had been a desperate policy, for only her life had stood between England and chaos. At first, there had been no heir to the throne who could win general acceptance. Then there had been the long crisis over Mary Queen of Scots. In the end, she had been justified. Gradually, a successor emerged who could satisfy most people: Mary's son, James VI of Scotland. For years, Elizabeth had subsidized him, but she had never said he should be her heir. She kept as silent as ever.

Increasingly, Cecil and others round Elizabeth came to support James's claim. They preferred him to his cousin, Lady Arbella Stuart, daughter of Darnley's younger brother. The fact of his already being a king commended him, and, after so many years of feminine rule, they hankered after a man. The Catholic claim had now passed to the Infanta Isabel, daughter of Philip II. Cecil's answer to that was to work to split and weaken Catholic opinion in England.

Old age had done nothing to fuddle Elizabeth's always keen wits. She knew perfectly well what Cecil was doing behind her back. Once she wrote sharply to James, "I marvel much to have such a subject that would impart so great a cause to you afore ever making me privy thereof." Beyond this, she let matters take their course. It was becoming increasingly clear that James was, in truth, the only acceptable person, As for what James would be like as a king, that was another matter. In an earlier letter, she had remarked to him, "I see well we two be of very different natures."

It was in 1601 that Elizabeth made what were to be her last great public speeches. Addressing a deputation of the

House of Commons, she made what was to be known for many years afterwards as her "Golden Speech". She spoke without a text. All through her life, Elizabeth's written style was elaborate to the point of being difficult to understand. The more she "improved" her work, the more tortuous it became. It was when she stood up and spoke, and felt, like the superlative actress that she was, the thrill of an audience, that she rose to heights that made her a worthy contemporary of Shakespeare and Marlowe. She said,

"I do assure you there is no prince that loves his subjects better, or whose love can countervail our love. There is no jewel, be it of never so rich a price, which I set before this jewel: I mean your love. . . . And, though God hath raised me high, yet I count this the glory of my crown, that I have reigned with your loves. . . .

"Of myself I must say this: I never was any greedy, scraping grasper, nor a strait, fast-holding Prince, nor yet a waster. My heart was never set on any worldly goods, but only for my subjects' good. What you bestow on me, I will not hoard it up, but receive it to bestow on you again. . . .

"There will never Queen sit in my seat with more zeal to my country, care for my subjects, and that will sooner with willingness venture her life for your good and safety, than myself. For it is my desire to live nor reign no longer than my life and reign shall be for your good. And though you have had and may have many princes more mighty and wise sitting in this seat, yet you never had nor shall have any more careful and loving."

This was Elizabeth at her difficult best; a fusion of intellect and personality. It was one of those moments when this strangely withdrawn and secretive woman became entirely out-going, and a strong tide of love flowed between her and her people. It is significant that it was this quality, not all her undoubted cleverness and her striking personality, that she herself wished to stress when she gave this account of the stewardship of her reign. Only three weeks later, she spoke her last words in public,

"This testimony I would have you carry hence for the world to know: that your Sovereign is more careful of your conservation than of herself, and will daily crave of God that they that wish you best may never wish in vain."

Elizabeth lived into her seventieth year, at that time a much more unusual feat than it is nowadays. Unlike many other great figures of her age, she was not granted a noble, spectacular death. Instead, as the end approached, she lay, low on a pile of cushions, huddled into herself like an animal that has been wounded. She would take no medicine and refused to eat. So strong had been her authority that there was nobody, even now, who was able to make her. A short while before, her coronation ring had had to be sawn off her finger. It was almost as if, that having been done, she had decided her life with England was over and she was willing herself to die.

Archbishop Whitgift was with her, but it is impossible to say what spiritual comfort she drew from him. She had fought with unshakeable courage for a Church that was moderate, ordered and decent. Did her thoughts in those moments turn to the greater religious virtues of faith and love? No one can say, except for "the only Ruler of Princes".

It was only when the end seemed inevitable that the Lord Admiral, he who had commanded the fleet against the Armada, asked her about her successor. After all the long years of silence she spoke. "I told you my seat hath been the seat of kings, and I will have no rascal to succeed me; and who should succeed me but a King." When Cecil asked whom she meant, she said, "Whom but our cousin of Scotland? I pray you trouble me no more." Next day, Cecil asked her again if she consented to James taking the crown. This time, she could only raise her hands in assent.

It was early in the morning of March 24th 1603, that Elizabeth Tudor died. She was buried in Westminster Abbey beside her half-sister, Mary. All that remains is the effigy on her tomb, brooding, a little enigmatic, as if she would mock with Hamlet, "You would pluck out the heart of my mystery."

Nobody has understood her completely because, in such a public life, she said so very little about herself. We know that she was, without any doubt, one of the most complex and contradictory characters ever to play a great part in history. She was very cautious, yet her whole reign was based on an almost reckless gamble on her own safety. She hated bloodshed and violence, yet at moments she was a triumphant, heroic figure of whom Henry IV of France exclaimed, "She only is a king! She only knows how to rule!" She was selfish and demanding in many personal relationships, but with her household servants, with a man like Burghley, with the people of England at large, she inspired and returned the warmth of a genuine human affection. Intellectual, super-subtle, the finely-worked product of her Renaissance education, she could talk to the keenest minds of her day upon equal terms. She also inspired an illiterate carter to say of her, "Now I see that the Queen is a woman as well as my wife." Her vulgarities, her ostentation, her vanity were as much a part of her as her financial skill, her scholarship, and her genius as a diplomat.

For many years after her death, and indeed right up to the present day, Englishmen looked back on her reign as a moment when their country was at its greatest. In a world of violence, intolerance, and cruelty in the name of religion, she consistently tried to establish order and peace, and to allow other people to get on with their own lives. But hers was no passive and sterile peace. She could recognize and stimulate excellence in her subjects to the very highest degree. For a short space of time, some of them were drawn into achievements beyond what seems like the normal peak of human ability.

    She was a very great queen.

Notes to Table

(1) The royal families of England and Spain were connected by their descent from John of Gaunt, third son of Edward III of England. The Spanish royal family were descendants of his second marriage and the English royal family of his third. Elizabeth and Philip of Spain stood in exactly the same relationship to Edward III.

(2) This table shows most of the people connected with the struggle for power in England and Scotland. Several other important characters can be fitted on to it.

Alençon, Elizabeth's suitor, was the youngest brother of Francis II of France, Mary Queen of Scots' first husband. Their sister Elisabeth, Mary's childhood friend, is shown on the table as Philip's II's third wife.

Don Carlos, whom Mary Queen of Scots once thought to marry, was Philip's son by his first marriage.

The Earl of Moray was the illegitimate son of James V of Scotland.

The Earl of Leicester was Lady Jane Grey's brother-in-law, and was step-father to the Earl of Essex.

(3) The following people shown on the table were claimants to the English throne:

After Edward's death: Lady Jane Grey (Protestant).

In Elizabeth's reign: Mary Queen of Scots and Philip II of Spain (Catholic); Lady Catherine Grey (Protestant).

Towards the end of Elizabeth's life: The Infanta Isabel (Catholic) and James VI of Scotland (Protestant), also Lady Arbella, or Arabella, Stuart.

(4) The present Queen, Elizabeth II, is a direct descendant of James I and VI.

THE ELIZABETHAN WORLD

It is still possible for somebody living in England to get a good idea of what the everyday world looked like to the Elizabethans.

(1) *Pictures*.

Elizabeth's parents and their generation were painted and drawn by Holbein. There was no one painter of such outstanding skill at Elizabeth's Court, but a large number of portraits survive. The Tudor section of the National Portrait Gallery, Charing Cross Road, London W.C.2, has portraits of nearly everybody mentioned in this book. The Victoria and Albert Museum, Cromwell Road, London S.W.7, has some very delightful miniatures by Elizabethan painters. The Scottish characters in Elizabeth's story can be found pictured in the Scottish National Portrait Gallery, Queen Street, Edinburgh.

Many great country houses, such as Hatfield, Woburn and Longleat, also contain portraits of notable Elizabethans. Paintings of this period pay great attention to details of costume.

(2) *Places associated with Elizabeth*.

Most of the great Tudor palaces, such as Greenwich, where she was born, and Nonsuch, have disappeared. The best place for realizing the magnificent scale on which she lived is now Hampton Court. It is still possible to visit the temporary residence of Elizabeth, and so many of her contemporaries; the Tower of London. She is buried in Westminster Abbey.

There are a number of places in Scotland associated with Mary, such as Linlithgow Palace, the ruins of her birthplace; Stirling Castle and the nearby church; Holyrood House; and Lochleven Castle. Mary, too, now lies in Westminster Abbey.

(3) *Other Elizabethan Houses*.

Many Elizabethan houses can still be visited. One of the finest is Burghley House in Huntingdonshire, built for Lord Burghley. Hardwick Hall in Derbyshire was built for the Countess of

Shrewsbury who helped to guard Mary Queen of Scots. Montacute House in Somerset is a fine example of an Elizabethan stone house, while Little Moreton Hall in Cheshire shows Tudor half-timbered building. Buckland Abbey near Plymouth has relics of the great seamen. These are all great country houses; much smaller Elizabethan houses can be seen in a town like Stratford-upon-Avon where there is Shakespeare's birthplace, Harvard House and Anne Hathaway's cottage.

This list is by no means complete. In most parts of England it is possible to catch glimpses of what the world of the Elizabethans was like: from small houses in market towns, from old farmhouses and barns, from the monuments in parish churches.

(4) *Literature.*

The other way of understanding the Elizabethans is to read their own works. Shakespeare gives the most complete picture of the age. Spenser, in *The Faerie Queene*, brings in portraits of Elizabeth and Mary Queen of Scots along with a great deal else. Elizabethan lyric poetry, much of which was simply the words of their popular songs, can be found in many anthologies such as *The Oxford Book of Sixteenth Century Verse* ed. E. K. Chambers (O.U.P.) and *The Poetry of the Age of Shakespeare* ed. W. T. Young (C.U.P.).

BOOKS

Below is a selection of books in which various points raised in this biography can be studied in more detail.

BIOGRAPHIES

Hester W. Chapman: *The Last Tudor King*, a Study of Edward VI (Cape)

Antonia Fraser: *Mary Queen of Scots* (Weidenfeld & Nicolson)

P. M. Handover: *The Second Cecil*, Sir Robert Cecil, later 1st Earl of Salisbury (Eyre & Spottiswoode)

(ed.) G. B. Harrison: *The Letters of Queen Elizabeth I* (Cassell)

N. Lloyd Williams: *Sir Walter Ralegh* (Eyre & Spottiswoode)

J. E. Neale: *Queen Elizabeth I* (Cape)

Lord Eustace Percy: *John Knox* (Hodder & Stoughton)

H. M. F. Prescott: *Spanish Tudor*, the Life of Bloody Mary (Constable)

A. L. Rowse: *Ralegh and the Throckmortons* (Macmillan)

Lytton Strachey: *Elizabeth and Essex* (Chatto & Windus)

Milton Waldman: *Elizabeth and Leicester* (Collins)

Evelyn Waugh: *Edmund Campion* (Longmans)

C. V. Wedgwood: *William the Silent* (Cape)

POLITICAL BACKGROUND

Lacey Baldwin Smith: *Elizabethan Epic* (Panther)

(ed.) S. T. Bindoff, J. Hurstfield and C. H. Williams: *Elizabethan Government and Society*, Essays Presented to Sir John Neale (University of London Press)

S. T. Bindoff: *Tudor England* (Penguin)

J. B. Black: *The Reign of Elizabeth* (Oxford University Press)

J. E. Neale: *Queen Elizabeth I and her Parliaments. Volume I 1559–1581; Volume II 1584–1601* (Cape)

Conyers Read: *Mr Secretary Walsingham and the Policy of Queen Elizabeth* (O.U.P. 3 volumes)

—— *Mr Secretary Cecil and Queen Elizabeth* (Cape)

A. L. Rowse: *The Expansion of Elizabethan England* (Macmillan)

SOCIAL HISTORY

J. Dover Wilson: *Life in Shakespeare's England* (Cambridge University Press and Pelican)

M. St. Clair Byrne: *Elizabethan Life in Town and Country* (Methuen and University Paperbacks)

G. M. Trevelyan: *English Social History* (Longmans)

THE ARTS

(ed.) Norman Ault: *Elizabethan Lyrics* (Longman)
(ed.) Alan Boase: *The Poetry of France*, Volume I 1400–1600 (Methuen)
(ed.) Paul Ganz: *The Paintings of Holbein* (Phaidon)
James Laver: *A Concise History of Costume* (Thames & Hudson)
James Emerson Philips: *Images of a Queen*, Mary Queen of Scots in Contemporary Literature (University of California Press)

SEAFARERS

Richard Hakluyt: *Voyages and Documents*, ed. Janet Hampton (O.U.P.)
Michael Lewis: *The Hawkins Dynasty* (George Allen and Unwin)
Garrett Mattingly: *The Defeat of the Spanish Armada* (Cape)
A. L. Rowse: *Sir Richard Grenville of the Revenge* (Macmillan)
J. A. Williamson: *The Age of Drake* and *Hawkins of Plymouth* (A. & C. Black)
—— *Sir Francis Drake* (Collins)

RELIGION

Dom Gregory Dix: *The Shape of the Liturgy* (Dacre Press)
Maurice Powicke: *The Reformation in England* (O.U.P.)

FOR YOUNGER READERS

Jacynth Hope-Simpson: *They Sailed from Plymouth* (Hamish Hamilton)
Margaret Irwin: Novels, *Young Bess* and *Elizabeth, Captive Princess* (Chatto & Windus)
(ed.) John Langdon Davis: *Elizabeth I* and *Mary Queen of Scots* (Jackdaw Publications, Cape)
Duncan Taylor: *The Elizabethan Age* (Dobson)